The Short Sale

A Framework for How Commercial Short Sales Are Actually Approved

James R. Calder

The Commercial Real Estate Systems Series

Shepherd Works Press

Copyright

The scenarios, structures, and examples discussed in this book are illustrative only and should not be interpreted as guarantees of outcome or suitability for any particular situation.

The CRE Short Sale

How Commercial Distress Is Actually Resolved—Before Foreclosure

This book is for informational and educational purposes only. It does not constitute legal, tax, accounting, or investment advice. Readers should consult their own professional advisors before acting on any information contained herein.

Published by **Shepherd Works Publishing**

This book is part of *The Commercial Real Estate Systems Series* by James R. Calder.

Shepherd Works Press is an imprint of Shepherd Works Publishing.

ISBN: 979-8-9944616-9-3

Printed in the United States of America

Library of Congress Control Number: TBD

Disclaimer

This book is provided for informational and educational purposes only. It does not constitute legal advice, tax advice, financial advice, investment advice, or a recommendation regarding any specific transaction, strategy, or course of action.

Commercial real estate transactions—particularly distressed asset resolutions—are complex and fact-specific. Laws, regulations, lender practices, tax consequences, and market conditions vary by jurisdiction and change over time. Readers should consult qualified legal, tax, accounting, and financial professionals before engaging in any transaction or relying on any information contained in this book.

The author and publisher make no representations or warranties, express or implied, regarding the accuracy, completeness, or applicability of the information contained herein and disclaim any liability for losses or damages arising from its use.

Nothing in this book creates a fiduciary relationship, advisory relationship, or professional obligation between the author, publisher, and the reader. Decisions based on this material are made at the reader's sole discretion and risk.

Distressed Transaction Notice

Distressed commercial real estate transactions—including loan workouts, short sales, negotiated payoffs, and deficiency resolutions—often involve heightened legal, tax, regulatory, and reputational risk. Outcomes depend on lender discretion, contractual language, borrower conduct, and jurisdiction-specific law.

The scenarios, structures, and examples discussed in this book are illustrative only and should not be interpreted as guarantees of outcome or suitability for any particular situation.

Important Notice & Intended Use

This book is intended for informational and educational purposes only.

The material presented reflects general principles and process frameworks related to commercial real estate distress resolution. It does not constitute legal, tax, accounting, investment, or financial advice, nor is it intended to substitute for professional judgment tailored to specific facts or circumstances.

Commercial real estate transactions—particularly those involving distressed assets, debt resolution, or negotiated outcomes—are inherently complex and fact-specific. Outcomes depend on market conditions, lender policies, governing documents, jurisdictional law, and the actions of third parties beyond the author's control.

Readers are strongly encouraged to consult qualified legal, tax, accounting, and financial professionals before implementing any strategy, structure, or transaction described in this book.

Neither the author nor the publisher makes any representation or warranty, express or implied, regarding the accuracy, completeness, or applicability of the information contained herein, and expressly disclaims any liability for actions taken or not taken based on this material.

This book does not advocate any specific transaction, investment, or course of action. It is designed to illuminate process, discipline, and decision-making considerations—not to prescribe outcomes.

Table of Contents

Dedication

To my Triune God—Father, Son, and Holy Spirit—from whom all wisdom, discernment, and stewardship flow.

To those who understand that clarity matters more than optimism, discipline matters more than bravado, and resolution matters more than winning.

This work is for the professionals who choose certainty over noise and process over ego.

Acknowledgements

This work exists by the grace of God.

Any clarity reflected in these pages—any insistence on discernment over impulse, structure over improvisation, and stewardship over ego—flows from that foundation.

Professionally, this book was shaped through years of observing how distressed commercial transactions actually resolve. Not as they are marketed. Not as they are explained afterward. But as they unfold inside institutions, across capital stacks, and under constraints that do not bend to intent or effort.

I am grateful to the lenders, servicers, attorneys, advisors, and operators whose standards, systems, and unwillingness to indulge avoidable risk revealed how resolution truly works—often quietly, often imperfectly, and rarely the way participants expect.

Any insight found here is a result of that exposure.
Any errors, omissions, or misjudgments are mine alone.

Preface

Why This Book Exists

Commercial real estate distress is widely discussed—and poorly understood.

Most commentary focuses on assets: vacancies, rent declines, obsolescence, cycles. Others focus on opportunity: discounts, dislocation, capital on the sidelines. Very little attention is paid to the actual mechanism through which distress is resolved—or fails to be resolved—inside lending institutions, capital stacks, and legal frameworks.

This book exists to correct that imbalance.

Commercial real estate distress is not primarily a real estate problem. It is a debt problem that surfaces in real assets. Buildings rarely fail suddenly. Capital structures fail quietly, mechanically, and predictably—often long before distress becomes visible to the market.

When resolution fails, it is rarely because value could not be preserved. It is because timing, structure, incentives, and process were misunderstood—or ignored.

This book was written to explain how commercial distress is actually resolved in the real world, before foreclosure becomes inevitable.

Who This Book Is For

This is not a book for casual observers of distressed markets.

It is written for:

- Buyers who value certainty over theatrics
- Operators who understand that execution risk destroys more value than pricing errors
- Lenders and servicers who must defend decisions under scrutiny
- Advisors who want transactions to close, not merely advance
- Capital that seeks repeatable access, not one-off outcomes

If your approach to distress is driven by headlines, optimism, or cleverness, this book will feel uncomfortable. That is intentional.

What This Book Is (and Is Not)

This is not a crisis manual.

It is not a market-timing thesis.

It is not a playbook for extracting advantage from weakness.

It is an operating system for resolution.

Every chapter exists because transactions routinely fail at that point. Every framework reflects how lenders, servicers, borrowers, and buyers actually behave under pressure—not how they claim to behave in theory.

The emphasis throughout is not on winning negotiations, but on removing friction. Not on maximizing price, but on ensuring closure. Not on speed for its own sake, but on disciplined sequencing that preserves optionality.

A Note on Perspective

Throughout this book, chapters are written from specific perspectives—lender, borrower, buyer, or resolution operator—not because roles are rigid, but because incentives are.

In practice, one party may occupy multiple roles. A borrower may also become the buyer. A buyer may act as the resolution operator. A lender may be constrained by policy while seeking flexibility in outcome.

Understanding these perspectives is not about empathy. It is about predictability.

Resolution succeeds when incentives are aligned and failure points are neutralized before they surface. It fails when parties assume shared understanding where none exists.

How This Book Should Be Used

This book is designed to be read sequentially once—and referenced repeatedly.

Each chapter builds on the prior one. Skipping ahead without internalizing the structure that precedes it will cause later sections to be misapplied. Distressed resolution is unforgiving of shortcuts.

Used properly, this book will:

- Help you eliminate non-closable deals early
- Reduce wasted time, capital, and credibility
- Improve lender access and internal sponsorship
- Increase certainty of execution
- Turn resolution skill into repeatable opportunity

Nothing in these pages is theoretical. Everything is designed to survive:

- Credit committees
- Legal review
- Tax scrutiny
- Regulatory oversight
- And reality

The Central Thesis

Commercial real estate distress is permanent because mispriced debt is permanent.

The opportunity does not lie in distress itself, but in disciplined resolution.

This book exists to teach that discipline.

— *James R. Calder*

Introduction

What You're Actually Looking At

This is not a book about distressed real estate.

It is a book about how commercial distress is resolved—or fails to be resolved—inside institutions, capital structures, and legal frameworks long before foreclosure becomes visible to the market.

Most people encounter commercial distress too late. By the time assets are marketed as "distressed," value has already leaked, narratives have hardened, attorneys are involved, and optionality has collapsed. What remains is not resolution—it is liquidation.

This book focuses on the phase before that happens.

It is about the quiet, procedural, often uncomfortable work of recognizing misalignment early, navigating institutional incentives, and converting deteriorating capital structures into controlled outcomes. It is about understanding where deals actually die—and how a small number of disciplined operators prevent that from happening.

This Is a Process Book, Not a Deal Book

You will not find deal stories here.

There are no heroic turnarounds, dramatic confrontations, or clever tactics. Those stories are entertaining, but they are misleading. They suggest that outcomes are driven by brilliance or courage.

They are not.

In commercial distress, outcomes are driven by:

- timing,
- documentation,
- incentive alignment,
- narrative control,

- and execution discipline.

This book is structured around those realities. Every chapter exists because that step regularly determines whether a transaction closes—or quietly disappears.

Why Foreclosure Is the Wrong Reference Point

Most discussions of distress implicitly assume foreclosure is the default outcome. It is not.

Foreclosure is a process failure, not a preference. It is what happens when:

- misalignment is ignored,
- resolution is delayed,
- narratives harden,
- and institutional momentum replaces discretion.

Foreclosure is slow, expensive, public, and value-destructive. Lenders do not choose it because it is optimal. They choose it because alternatives were not structured early enough—or credibly enough—to survive scrutiny.

This book is about those alternatives.

The Role of the Resolution Operator

Throughout this book, you will see the term resolution operator. This is intentional.

A resolution operator is not defined by title. It is defined by function.

A resolution operator is the party—sometimes a buyer, sometimes a borrower, sometimes an advisor—who:

- understands how distress is recognized internally,
- anticipates where resistance will surface,
- aligns stakeholders before pressure peaks,
- and removes friction before it becomes fatal.

Resolution operators do not argue markets.

They do not pressure committees.

They do not "win" negotiations.

They structure outcomes that become easier to approve than to delay.

This book teaches that posture.

What Makes Commercial Short Sales Different

Commercial short sales are often misunderstood because they are mistakenly compared to residential ones.

They are not analogous.

Commercial short sales:

- are evaluated institutionally, not emotionally,
- require defensibility, not sympathy,
- hinge on consent hierarchies, not single decisions,
- and succeed or fail based on process survivability, not pricing alone.

They are not opportunistic by nature. They are corrective mechanisms within leveraged systems that have drifted out of alignment.

This book treats them accordingly.

What You Will Learn

By the time you reach the end of this book, you will understand:

- why most distressed deals should never be pursued,
- how lenders actually recognize impairment,
- how approval narratives are formed and defended,
- where execution risk really lives,
- why certainty consistently defeats price,
- how stakeholder consent is obtained—or neutralized,
- and how disciplined resolution creates repeatable access.

You will also understand why most participants—buyers, borrowers, and advisors alike—fail at this work despite good intentions.

How to Read What Follows

This book is sequential by design.

Each chapter removes a specific failure mode. Skipping steps or treating chapters as standalone tactics will cause later sections to be misapplied. Distressed resolution is cumulative. Early errors cannot be corrected downstream.

Read it once straight through.
Then return to it as a reference.

Nothing here is theoretical. Everything is written to survive credit committees, legal review, tax scrutiny, and time.

A Final Orientation

If you are looking for speed, this book will frustrate you.
If you are looking for certainty, it will resonate.

Resolution is not dramatic.
It is deliberate.

And it begins with understanding what you are actually solving.

What follows is not a collection of tactics or case studies. It is a structural examination of how commercial distress actually unfolds—and how it is resolved when discipline replaces denial.

The first step is not sourcing. It is not negotiation. It is not pricing.

It is understanding why distress exists at all, how it is misdiagnosed, and why most participants respond too late.

That is where this work begins.

Chapter 1: Why Structured Resolution Matters

Commercial Real Estate, Mispriced Debt, and the Role of Discipline

Primary Perspective: Resolution Operator
Secondary Perspectives: Lender / Servicer, Buyer
Reader Objective: Understand why commercial real estate distress is driven by mispriced debt—not asset failure—and why negotiated resolution is a permanent requirement across market cycles.

> *Note*: In many commercial short sales, the borrower and buyer may ultimately be the same economic entity. This book treats them as separate perspectives because lenders evaluate them as distinct roles, each with different incentives, risks, and credibility thresholds.

Orientation: Why This Chapter Exists

Most people misunderstand commercial real estate distress.
They assume assets fail first and debt fails second.

In practice, the opposite is almost always true.

Commercial real estate distress is a debt problem that surfaces in real assets—and resolution succeeds or fails based on whether that reality is recognized early or denied until options collapse.

If this distinction is not internalized, everything that follows will be misread as tactics rather than structure—deal-making rather than resolution.

This chapter exists to establish that foundation.

The Resolution Operator's Frame

A resolution operator does not begin with the building.

They do not ask:

- Is this a good asset?
- Will rents recover?
- Is the sponsor optimistic?

Those questions are secondary.

The primary questions are:

- Is the debt aligned with current economic reality?
- Can that misalignment be corrected through time?
- If not, can it be corrected through negotiation?
- If neither, what fails next—and who absorbs the loss?

From this perspective, distress is not dramatic.

It is mechanical.

Rates change.

Cap rates move.

Liquidity contracts.

Operating costs rise.

Loan terms do not.

When the math no longer works, time stops being an ally and becomes a liability.

> *In distressed environments, outcomes are governed less by price than by what a lender can defend and execute.*

That idea will matter later.

For now, it explains why denial is so expensive.

Where Distress Is Commonly Misread

Borrowers: Distress as Temporary

Borrowers often assume:

- rates will fall,
- lenders will extend,
- markets will recover in time.

This belief delays engagement and increases loss severity.

Buyers: Distress as Opportunity

Buyers frequently see distress and think:

- discounted price,
- motivated seller,
- mispriced asset.

Without understanding the debt, they misprice execution risk—and lose deals they believed they had won.

Lenders: Delay as Neutral

Lenders sometimes assume:

- more time preserves value,
- forbearance is neutral,
- foreclosure remains optional.

In the current environment, delay often destroys optionality.

What Actually Happens in the Real World

Distressed commercial assets rarely collapse suddenly.

Instead:

- loans mature,
- refinance gaps appear,
- equity becomes unavailable,
- extensions turn conditional,
- interest-rate caps expire,
- carrying costs rise quietly.

Assets may continue operating while the capital structure fails.

By the time foreclosure becomes visible, value has already leaked.

Resolution rarely fails abruptly. It erodes through delay, denial, and unchallenged assumptions.

Failure Path vs. Success Path

Failure Path

- Distress is denied
- Time is treated as strategy
- Borrower resists reality
- Lender delays escalation
- Foreclosure bias builds
- Value destruction accelerates

Success Path

- Debt misalignment is acknowledged early
- Impairment becomes defensible
- Stakeholders engage while options exist
- Resolution occurs before foreclosure momentum
- Loss is contained
- The asset is reset productively

The difference is not intelligence. It is timing, discipline, and early acceptance of constraint.

The Central Problem Is Debt, Not Real Estate

Commercial real estate does not fail the way most people think it does.

Buildings do not disappear overnight.
Tenants do not vanish uniformly.
Demand does not collapse all at once.

What fails—repeatedly and predictably—is debt structure that cannot adapt to changing economic conditions.

Commercial real estate distress occurs when capital terms no longer align with asset cash flow, regardless of asset quality.

This mismatch is permanent in leveraged real assets:

- interest rates move,
- cap rates change,
- liquidity tightens,
- costs rise,
- time advances.

Debt remains fixed.

Why the Current Cycle Makes This Unavoidable

The present CRE cycle removes the ability to ignore this reality.

Hundreds of billions of dollars in commercial real estate debt are maturing under assumptions that no longer hold:

- low interest rates,
- abundant refinancing liquidity,
- compressed cap rates,
- inexpensive extensions,
- minimal equity requirements.

For many sponsors, the problem is simple:

The value required to refinance no longer exists, and the equity required to bridge the gap is unavailable—or unwilling.

It is arithmetic.

Why "Holding On" No Longer Works

In prior cycles, time was often neutral or favorable.

Sponsors could:

- extend loans,
- refinance with modest equity,
- wait for rate relief,

- rely on lender forbearance.

In the current environment, time is often destructive:

- interest-rate caps expire,
- carry costs rise,
- insurance and taxes increase,
- deferred maintenance compounds,
- tenant demand shifts unevenly.

Each month of delay narrows options for all parties involved.

Foreclosure Is a Structural Failure, Not a Preference

Foreclosure is not a lender's preferred outcome.

Across cycles, foreclosure is:

- slow,
- expensive,
- public,
- uncertain,
- litigation-prone,
- value-destructive.

Lenders choose foreclosure only when negotiated resolution fails.

Foreclosure is not strategy.

It is process failure.

That failure creates the opening for structured resolution.

The Role of Commercial Short Sales

A commercial short sale is not:

- a bailout,
- a fire sale,
- a moral judgment,
- or a speculative tactic.

It is a resolution mechanism.

Properly structured, it:

- acknowledges economic reality,
- limits loss severity,
- avoids litigation and public process,
- preserves reputations,
- clears impaired debt,
- resets the asset for productive use.

Short sales are not opportunistic by nature.

They are corrective.

Why This Is Always Relevant

The current cycle increases volume and urgency—but not relevance.

Commercial short sales exist in every environment because the following are permanent:

- fragile capital stacks,
- sponsor-specific failure,
- asset obsolescence,
- execution errors,
- and time itself.

Markets change the volume of short sales, not the structural reasons they occur.

Why Most Participants Fail

Most market participants fail at structured resolution because they:

- focus on price instead of process,
- underestimate legal and tax complexity,
- ignore lender psychology,
- lack patience and discipline,
- try to "win" negotiations instead of resolve them.

This is not a volume strategy.

It is a precision discipline.

Why Disciplined Resolution Capital Is Rare

Most capital is optimized for:

- growth,
- speed,
- momentum,
- narrative.

Resolution requires:

- patience,
- legal fluency,
- tax awareness,
- emotional neutrality,
- reputation sensitivity,
- process discipline.

That scarcity—not distress itself—is the source of durable advantage.

The Purpose of This Book

This book exists to answer one question:

How do you resolve mispriced commercial real estate debt in a way that actually closes—without destroying value, credibility, or future opportunity?

It is written for:

- operators, not tourists,
- buyers who value certainty over bravado,
- capital that understands process is leverage,
- professionals seeking repeatable access—not one-off wins.

This is not a crisis manual.

It is an operating system.

How to Read What Follows

The chapters that follow map the full lifecycle of a commercial short sale:

- deal selection,

- lender engagement,
- narrative control,
- negotiation and clearance,
- closing,
- post-close value creation.

Each chapter exists because deals routinely fail there.

Nothing in this book is theoretical.
Everything is designed to survive:

- credit committees,
- lawyers,
- CPAs,
- regulators,
- and reality.

Core Thesis

If there is one idea this book rests on, it is this:

> Commercial real estate distress is permanent because mispriced debt is permanent.

The opportunity is not distress.
It is disciplined resolution executed before options collapse.

The current cycle makes this urgent.
The structure makes it timeless.

Chapter 2: Market Context, Deal Selection & Kill Filters

Deciding What Is Worth Attempting

Primary Perspective: Buyer / Resolution Operator
Secondary Perspective: Lender
Reader Objective: Learn how to screen opportunities using lender behavior, capital-stack reality, and impairment signals—killing deals early that cannot close regardless of price.

Orientation: Why This Chapter Exists

Most failed short sales fail before a lender is ever engaged.

Not because of price.
Not because of documentation.
Not because of timing.

They fail because the deal never should have been pursued.

This chapter exists to impose discipline before momentum, emotion, or sunk cost override structural reality. It teaches how to determine—early—whether a transaction is structurally resolvable, or merely distressed in appearance.

This is the chapter that saves the most time, capital, and credibility.

The Resolution Operator's Frame

From a buyer's perspective, opportunity is abundant.

From a resolution operator's perspective, viable opportunity is scarce and identifiable early.

A resolution operator does not begin by asking:

- Is the seller motivated?
- Is the price attractive?

- Is the asset interesting?

Those are downstream questions.

The first questions are structural:

- Is the lender impaired or merely uncomfortable?
- Can the capital stack be cleared?
- Does timing favor resolution—or delay?
- Can a loss be defended internally by the lender?

If the answer to any of these is no, the deal is structurally non-viable at entry.

It is already dead.

This is where professional discipline diverges from amateur enthusiasm.

Where Deals Are Commonly Misread

Buyers: Distress ≠ Viability

Many buyers equate:

- late payments,
- maturity pressure,
- sponsor frustration,

with short-sale viability.

They are not the same.

A loan can be stressed without being impaired.
A sponsor can be desperate while a lender remains patient.
A poorly managed asset does not automatically justify loss.

Lenders: Silence ≠ Strategy

Some lenders interpret:

- borrower quiet,
- delayed communication,
- partial compliance,

as recoverable delay.

In reality, silence often means the borrower has no viable path forward—but has not yet accepted it.

This mismatch creates false positives that waste time on deals that never had a closing path.

What Actually Happens in Failed Deals

Failed deals follow a predictable arc:

- A distressed-looking opportunity surfaces
- Buyer engages enthusiastically
- Underwriting focuses on upside
- Assumptions drift toward stabilization
- Lender engagement is delayed or informal
- Impairment is never confirmed
- Approval authority is misidentified
- Momentum decays quietly

No rejection.
No explicit "no."
Just erosion through delay and loss of sponsorship.

By the time clarity arrives, credibility is already spent.

Failure Path vs. Success Path

Failure Path

- Sponsor distress is mistaken for lender distress
- Time is treated as strategy
- Capital structure is ignored early
- Impairment is assumed, not confirmed
- Complexity is discovered late

These deals fail late—which is the most expensive way to fail.

Success Path

- Distress is confirmed structurally, not emotionally
- Lender behavior signals openness to resolution
- Capital stack is mapped early
- Timing pressure is real and asymmetric
- Kill filters are applied without hesitation

Successful operators kill far more deals than they pursue.

That is not conservatism.

It is competence.

The Core Truth (Non-Negotiable)

If lender impairment is not acknowledged at entry, the short sale will fail regardless of buyer effort.

This chapter exists to prevent the pursuit of deals that cannot be approved, regardless of effort.

When Short Sales Exist (Macro Preconditions)

Short sales are not cyclical by default.

They occur when **four forces overlap**.

The Four Preconditions

1. Debt Stress

- Maturity walls
- Floating-rate resets
- Expiring interest-rate caps
- DSCR covenant breaches

2. Capital Exhaustion

- Sponsor unable or unwilling to inject equity
- Failed capital calls
- LP fatigue or revolt

3. Value Impairment

- As-is value below loan balance
- Cap-rate expansion
- Functional or economic obsolescence

4. Lender Incentive Alignment

- Foreclosure worse than negotiated loss
- Regulatory or reputational pressure
- Desire for clean resolution

If any one is missing, a short sale will not close.

Market Conditions That Support Short Sales

Short sales thrive in dislocated markets—not merely "down" markets.

Supportive Conditions

- Rapid rate increases
- Liquidity contraction
- Insurance cost spikes
- CapEx inflation
- Tenant demand shifts
- Asset-type obsolescence

Weak Conditions (Short Sales Rare)

- Gradual downturns
- Ample refinancing liquidity
- Rent growth masking debt stress
- Sponsor overcapitalization

Distress must be structural, not temporary.

Asset Classes: Where Short Sales Actually Work

Higher-Probability Asset Types

- Office (especially suburban / commodity)

- Retail with anchor risk
- Older industrial with deferred CapEx
- Select-service hospitality
- Mixed-use with broken capital stacks

Lower-Probability Asset Types

- Core multifamily (agency backstops)
- Trophy assets with sponsor support
- New construction with fresh equity
- Fully stabilized institutional assets

Short sales occur where **capital patience ends**, not where assets are weakest.

Lender Type Filter (More Important Than Asset Type)

A strong asset with the wrong lender is a dead deal.

Higher-Probability Lenders

- Regional and community banks
- Credit unions
- Balance-sheet lenders
- CMBS special servicers (with runway)

Lower-Probability Lenders

- Agencies (Fannie / Freddie)
- Life companies
- Relationship-driven private lenders
- Family offices with emotional capital

Rule:

If the lender does not recognize or cannot defend loss, there is no short sale.

Sponsor Behavior Filter (The Silent Killer)

Cooperative Indicators

- Transparent communication
- Willingness to share financials
- Acceptance of value reality
- Focus on guaranty relief
- Desire for finality

Non-Cooperative Red Flags

- "One more refi attempt"
- Blaming the lender exclusively
- Refusing third-party valuations
- Early litigation threats
- Withholding access or data

Non-cooperative sponsors destroy timelines and credibility.

Capital Stack Reality Check

Complexity is not fatal.

Unmanageable complexity is.

Acceptable Complexity

- One senior lender plus manageable juniors
- Clear lien positions
- Negotiable junior creditors

Fatal Complexity

- Multiple hostile juniors
- IRS liens with timing conflicts
- Opaque mezz structures
- Unresolved judgments
- Pending bankruptcy filings

If the capital stack cannot be cleared without coercion or litigation, Chapter 2 must kill it.

As-Is Value: The Hard Gate

Before engaging a lender, answer one question:

Can defensible as-is value plausibly justify a short payoff?

Only third-party reports that support loss defensibility reduce committee friction. All others increase scrutiny.

If the answer is no:

- walk immediately,
- do not "see if it works,"
- do not hope negotiation saves it.

Short sales are approved on defensible economics—not effort.

Timeline Reality Filter

Short sales require time and patience.

Minimum Viable Timelines

- 3–6 months (clean cases)
- 6–12 months (complex stacks / CMBS)

Kill If

- capital is impatient,
- investors require fast closes,
- foreclosure is imminent without standstill,
- carry costs exceed buffer.

It is the profit gate—and the credibility gate.

Reputational Risk Filter (Often Ignored)

Every failed short sale costs reputational capital.

Walk away if:

- the borrower is litigious,
- media exposure risk exists,
- regulatory scrutiny is elevated,
- political or municipal pressure is present,
- facts are messy or misrepresented.

You are building a long game.

The Kill Checklist (Non-Negotiable)

Kill the deal if **any** of the following are true:

- Lender unwilling to acknowledge impairment
- Sponsor denies reality
- As-is value cannot justify payoff
- Capital stack cannot be cleared
- Environmental risk is unbounded
- Timeline cannot be controlled
- Certainty of close does not exist at entry

No exceptions.

No heroics.

What "Done" Looks Like

When this chapter is executed correctly, you have:

- a deal that deserves effort,
- aligned lender behavior,
- a cooperative (or irrelevant) sponsor,
- defensible economics,
- a clear path through Chapters 3–12.

Everything else is noise.

Lifecycle Alignment

This chapter feeds every step that follows.

If it is wrong:

- Chapter 3 wastes time
- Chapter 4 never settles
- Chapter 5 stalls
- Chapter 6 retrades
- Chapter 7 collapses
- Chapter 8 never closes

This process is not optional.

It is the profit gate.

Chapter 3: Pre-Foreclosure Access & Bank / Servicer Entry

The Front Door to Commercial Short Sales

Primary Perspective: Lender / Servicer
Secondary Perspective: Buyer
Reader Objective: Understand how distressed CRE loans move through internal lender escalation—and how disciplined counterparties earn access *before foreclosure momentum becomes irreversible.*

Orientation: Why This Chapter Exists

Most buyers believe access to distressed deals is a sourcing problem.

It is not.

It is a trust and timing problem inside regulated institutions.

This chapter exists to establish a non-negotiable truth:

- Distress is not created by assets deteriorating—it is created by capital structures failing to adapt.
- Everything that follows depends on understanding that sequence correctly.

Pre-foreclosure access is not granted because a buyer is interested.
It is granted because a lender believes engagement reduces risk.

Once that is understood, access stops feeling mysterious—and becomes repeatable.

How Distress Looks from Inside a Bank or Servicer

Inside a bank or servicing platform, distress does not resemble opportunity.

It appears as:

- increased scrutiny,
- reporting burden,

- regulatory exposure,
- reputational risk.

A distressed loan represents work, not upside.

Special assets teams are not trying to:

- maximize price,
- run auctions,
- or entertain curiosity.

They are trying to:

- stabilize a deteriorating situation,
- document defensible decisions,
- and avoid outcomes that attract criticism later.

From this perspective, buyer engagement is **useful only if it:**

- shortens timelines,
- reduces uncertainty,
- and supports internal loss defensibility.

Access is therefore conditional, not open.

Where Buyers Commonly Misread the Situation

Outreach Is Not Sales

Many buyers approach lenders as if they are:

- marketing assets,
- shopping price,
- or soliciting bids.

This framing is backward.

At this stage, lenders are not sellers.

They are risk managers.

Any outreach that increases perceived work, risk, or scrutiny reduces access.

Silence Is Not Rejection

Lack of response is often interpreted as disinterest.

More often, it reflects:

- misaligned timing,
- incomplete internal escalation,
- or uncertainty about buyer credibility.

Pushing harder at this stage usually reduces access rather than improving it.

The Internal Lifecycle of a Distressed Loan

Understanding internal sequencing is critical to timing outreach correctly.

A typical distressed CRE loan follows this arc:

- Performance stress appears (DSCR, maturity risk, cap expiry)
- Monitoring remains quiet and procedural
- Borrower engagement becomes intermittent
- Escalation thresholds are approached
- Special assets involvement begins
- Resolution paths are evaluated internally

Buyer access usually occurs after escalation but before foreclosure bias sets in.

Buyers who appear too early are dismissed as noise.
Buyers who appear too late are treated as liquidation bidders.

The window between those states is narrow—and decisive.

Failure Path vs. Access Path

Failure Path

- Approaching lenders before internal escalation has occurred
- Increasing perceived workload or regulatory exposure
- Introducing uncertainty without offering process relief
- Signaling opportunism rather than containment
- Misreading institutional silence as negotiability

These approaches increase friction and reduce trust.

Access Path

- Outreach aligned with internal escalation timing
- Language that reflects lender constraints
- Emphasis on process, not price
- Demonstrated ability to close quietly and cleanly
- Respect for internal approval paths

Access is earned by reducing work, not creating it.

Core Operating Truth

> You do not 'find' commercial short sales.
>
> You are invited into them—when your presence reduces risk inside the institution.

This chapter is about earning that invitation.

Where Pre-Foreclosure Deals Actually Originate

The Myth

- "Banks publish pre-foreclosures"
- "Scrape default notices and call it a pipeline"

That works in residential.

It **does not work in** commercial real estate.

The Reality

CRE short-sale opportunities emerge from internal lender workflows long before anything is public.

Primary sources:

- Bank special assets / workout departments
- Credit union problem loan officers
- CMBS special servicers
- Borrowers already in technical default
- Brokers quietly shopping assets with lender awareness

- Attorneys, receivers, and turnaround professionals

Your job is to connect to 1–3 directly, and 4–6 indirectly.

Who You Actually Contact (Titles Matter)

Balance-Sheet Banks

Correct targets:

- Special Assets Officer
- Workout Officer
- Distressed Asset Manager
- Problem Loan Officer
- CRE Portfolio Manager

Avoid:

- Branch loan officers
- Relationship managers (without warm intro)
- Front-line analysts

Once distress begins, these roles do not control outcomes.

Credit Unions

Credit unions are:

- smaller,
- relationship-driven,
- often late to acknowledge impairment.

Correct targets:

- VP of Lending
- Chief Credit Officer (CCO)
- Senior Commercial Loan Officer

Speak capital preservation, not policy.

CMBS and Securitized Loans

This is a different game entirely.

If the loan is securitized:

- the "lender" does not decide,
- the special servicer controls the process,
- the PSA is the rulebook.

Correct targets:

- Special servicer asset manager
- Surveillance analyst (early stage)
- Occasionally the master servicer (pre-default only)

Expect:

- slower timelines,
- rigid documentation,
- committee approval,
- zero emotion.

What Triggers a Loan to Enter Workout

Knowing this determines when outreach works.

Common triggers:

- DSCR below covenant (often <1.20x)
- Debt yield below threshold (often <8–10%)
- Maturity without viable refinance
- Expired or unaffordable rate caps
- Missed tax or insurance payments
- Deferred maintenance threatening collateral
- Material tenant default

Many loans are in technical default long before payments stop.

Positioning: Where Most Buyers Fail

When lenders hear "short sale," they think:

- loss,
- litigation risk,

- regulatory scrutiny,
- reputation,
- time drain.

They do not think opportunity.

Your positioning must answer one question:

Why are you safer than foreclosure?

Your Actual Role

You are not a buyer.

You are a:

- resolution counterparty,
- focused on certainty and loss containment,
- willing to operate within lender constraints,
- not interested in retrades, embarrassment, or litigation.

If this is not true, do not outreach.

Outreach Strategy (Professional, Not Aggressive)

Optimal Entry Window

Stage	Visibility	Leverage
Pre-default	Low	High
Technical default	Medium	Medium
Post-default / NOD	High	Low

Best entry: technical default, pre-NOD.

Initial Outreach (Cold, Professional)

Subject: CRE Distressed Resolution – Buyer Capability Introduction

Hello [Name],

I'm reaching out to introduce our firm. We work with lenders and servicers on resolving underperforming commercial real estate loans through structured acquisitions and short-sale transactions when foreclosure is not the optimal outcome.

We focus on assets where maturity risk, DSCR pressure, or capital requirements have impaired collateral value, and where an orderly sale provides a faster, cleaner resolution than REO.

I'm not calling on a specific asset today—only to understand your process and be available as a qualified counterparty when alternatives are evaluated.

Happy to provide background, proof of funds, and references if helpful.

Best regards,

[Name]

Why this works:

- no fishing,
- no pressure,
- no asset request,
- signals seriousness.

Follow-Up Cadence

- Day 0: Initial email
- Day 5–7: Polite follow-up
- Day 21: Value-add touch (market insight, not a pitch)
- Quarterly: Light check-in

One response puts you on the radar.

What They Can—and Cannot—Share

They Can Share

- General asset type
- Market
- Loan balance range
- Stage of distress
- Process timing
- Whether alternatives are being considered

They Cannot Share

- Borrower financials
- Exact default status
- Internal valuations
- Competing buyer details

Pressure equals blacklist.

Your Credibility Kit (Non-Optional)

Before outreach, you must have:

- one-page firm overview,
- clearly defined asset focus,
- geographic scope,
- real proof of funds,
- execution partners (PM, GC, legal),
- track record or operator experience,
- explicit non-retrade posture.

If you cannot demonstrate certainty of close, do not initiate contact.

Intake & Early Kill Screen

The moment an asset is mentioned, log it.

Required intake:

- lender / servicer
- contact
- asset type and location
- loan balance
- approximate NOI
- distress stage
- timing sensitivity
- capital stack complexity
- borrower cooperation

Kill immediately if:

- environmental risk is unbounded,
- title defects are incurable,
- political or zoning exposure exists,
- borrower is hostile and litigious,
- CMBS has zero flexibility and no upside.

Walking early builds reputation.

Standstill & Forbearance: Leading Indicator

If a lender is open to:

- standstill,
- forbearance,
- extended workout,

they want resolution.

These agreements buy time for:

- packaging,
- buyer sourcing,
- negotiation.

They are among the strongest indicators of short-sale viability.

What "Done" Looks Like

When this chapter is executed correctly, you have:

- named contacts at banks, credit unions, and servicers,
- a clean outreach script that does not burn bridges,
- a ready credibility kit,
- a live intake tracker,
- early visibility into distressed loans,
- a reputation as serious, professional, low-drama.

This is the front end of the funnel.

Everything else depends on it.

Chapter 4: Distress Confirmation & Control of the Narrative

Where Short Sales Become Possible—or Die Quietly

Primary Perspective: Lender
Secondary Perspectives: Borrower / Guarantor, Buyer
Reader Objective: Understand how lenders recognize impairment, frame internal narratives, and decide whether resolution or foreclosure is the defensible path.

Orientation: Why This Chapter Exists

No commercial short sale closes until the lender formally recognizes impairment.
That recognition does not occur because a borrower is struggling, a buyer offers a discount, or markets weaken.
It occurs when a lender concludes—internally—that continuing forward creates greater risk than resolving now.

Distress is not a feeling.
It is an institutional determination that must be defensible, documented, and survivable under review.

Most transactions fail here without rejection. They stall until foreclosure becomes the default path.
This chapter explains how impairment becomes real inside a lender—and why controlling that narrative determines whether resolution remains possible.

How Lenders Define "Distress" (What It Actually Means)

Distress is not the same as default.

A loan can be:

- current on payments,
- technically compliant,
- and still unresolvable.

Distress is confirmed when at least one of the following becomes provable:

- **Maturity failure**: The loan cannot be refinanced at maturity under current market terms without new equity.
- **Inability to cure**: The borrower cannot inject capital to cure covenants, fund CapEx, or stabilize performance.
- **Collateral impairment**: As-is value cannot support the debt, even under realistic stabilization.
- **Outcome comparison**: Foreclosure is expected to produce a worse recovery than a negotiated sale.

Until one of these is defensible, no short sale is approvable.

The Lender's Real Decision Standard

Declaring impairment is not a market call. It is a governance event.

Inside a regulated institution, impairment triggers accounting treatment, oversight, and a permanent decision record.

Lenders are not asking whether the borrower is stressed or the asset declined. They are asking one question:

> "If this decision is reviewed later—by auditors, regulators, investors, or a court—can we defend it?"

If the answer is unclear, action pauses.

Pausing is not neutral.

Pausing allows foreclosure momentum to take over.

The Three Questions Every Lender Must Answer

Every distressed loan must resolve three internal questions:

1. **Is the impairment real?**
   Not temporary. Not emotional. Not sponsor-driven.
2. **Is foreclosure worse?**

Time, cost, litigation risk, optics, and recovery uncertainty.

3. **Is the proposed resolution clean?**

   No retrades. No surprises. No lingering exposure.

If any answer is unclear, the lender stalls.

Stalling is not neutral.

Stalling becomes foreclosure by inertia.

Where Borrowers and Buyers Misread This

Borrowers: "It's Obvious"

Borrowers often believe distress is self-evident:

- cash flow is tight,
- refinancing failed,
- equity is gone.

From the lender's perspective, none of that is decisive until it's:

- documented,
- quantified,
- and defensible.

Buyers: "Price Proves It"

Buyers often assume:

- a low offer proves distress,
- comps speak for themselves,
- inevitability overrides process.

Price does not establish impairment.

Narrative does.

How Distress Gets Confirmed in the Real World

Distress recognition typically unfolds gradually:

- performance metrics weaken,
- borrower explanations repeat,

- "time will fix it" narratives thin,
- third-party data contradicts optimism,
- internal questions escalate,
- alternatives are modeled quietly.

Committees wait for clarity.

Servicers seek defensibility.

Lenders test assumptions.

Buyers who pressure the process usually trigger resistance.

Buyers who support internal reasoning—without forcing it—become useful.

Borrower Psychology (Predictable Archetypes)

Borrower behavior predicts outcomes more reliably than financial statements.

1. **The Denier**
   Expects rates, values, or lenders to change. Resists third-party validation.
   Resolution probability: Low
2. **The Frozen Sponsor**
   Accepts reality privately but avoids formal acknowledgment. Delays decisions.
   Resolution probability: Medium–Low
3. **The Strategic Resolver**
   Accepts loss, prioritizes guaranty relief and finality, cooperates fully.
   Resolution probability: High
4. **The Litigator**
   Escalates early, frames disputes emotionally or adversarially.
   Resolution probability: Near zero

The best short-sale candidates are not the most distressed borrowers.

They are the ones prepared to conclude the situation.

What borrowers actually care about is not price. It's:

- guaranty exposure and carve-outs,
- reputation,
- time and stress,
- finality.

If those are ignored, cooperation erodes.

Proving "Inability to Cure" (Non-Negotiable)

A short sale requires proof the borrower cannot fix the problem.

Acceptable commercial proof includes:

- failed refinance term sheets,
- credible appraisals showing impairment,
- projections with no realistic DSCR recovery,
- failed capital calls or LP refusal,
- sponsor liquidity statements,
- rate cap costs that break feasibility,
- CapEx requirements exceeding sponsor capacity.

This is not residential "hardship."

It is economic impossibility.

Red flags (kill early):

- borrower refuses data,
- "miracle refi" claims,
- exclusive blame narratives,
- refusal to discuss guaranty exposure.

These deals waste time and poison credibility.

Establishing As-Is Value Without Creating Resistance

In distress, value is not:

- original purchase price,
- loan balance,
- replacement cost,
- stabilized pro forma.

Value is market-clearing reality:

> What a qualified buyer will pay today for the asset as-is, with current leases, condition, and risk—without heroic assumptions.

Tools that support defensible value:

- distressed broker opinion of value,
- recent distressed comps,
- cost-to-cure and deferred maintenance schedules,
- lease rollover risk modeling.

Your job is to make value feel inevitable, not aggressive.

Controlling the Narrative (This Is the Win Condition)

The narrative that survives committee review is simple, unemotional, and repeatable:

"The asset is impaired due to structural market conditions and capital constraints.
Refinancing or cure is not viable without uneconomic equity.
Foreclosure increases time, cost, and uncertainty.
A negotiated sale at current market value provides certainty and minimizes loss severity."

Any narrative that emphasizes blame, upside, or buyer advantage introduces resistance.

Certainty—not opportunity—is what gets approved.

The Decision Fork: Short Sale vs Foreclosure

Lenders choose a short sale when:

- recovery timing is faster,
- loss severity is defensible,
- buyer credibility is strong,
- borrower cooperation persists,
- legal risk is contained.

Lenders choose foreclosure when:

- borrower obstructs,
- buyer credibility is weak,
- capital stack is hostile,
- CMBS constraints dominate,
- the narrative is unsettled.

This decision often happens silently.

If you're not shaping it, you're losing it.

Failure Modes (Where Deals Die Quietly)

Deals die here when:

- borrower goes dark,
- "value" feels opportunistic,
- buyer overplays leverage,
- lender feels exposed to scrutiny,
- inability-to-cure proof is weak,
- foreclosure counsel gains momentum.

Once foreclosure counsel takes over, optionality collapses.

What "Done" Looks Like

When this chapter is executed correctly, the lender has:

- acknowledged impairment (explicitly or implicitly),
- accepted foreclosure as inferior,
- aligned internally on value reality,
- and authorized formal packaging.

The clearest signal is not enthusiasm or urgency.

It is restraint.

The lender says—directly or through counsel:

> "Prepare and submit a complete package."

That instruction means resolution is now possible.

Chapter 5: How Lenders Actually Review Short Sale Packages

Why Most Files Stall—and What Survives Committee Scrutiny

Primary Perspective: Lender / Credit Committee
Secondary Perspective: Buyer / Resolution Operator
Reader Objective: Understand how short-sale submissions are evaluated internally, why most packages fail quietly, and how to construct a file that survives every approval layer.

Orientation: Why This Chapter Exists

Most short sales do not fail because of price, diligence, or documentation.

They fail because someone with veto authority was not identified—or not neutralized—before momentum formed.

This chapter exists to explain why stakeholder clearance is not administrative work, but structural risk control.
Until every veto holder is known and addressed, no deal is real.

The Governing Reality

A short sale package is not reviewed as a transaction.
It is reviewed as a decision record.

Credit committees are not evaluating creativity, upside, or effort.
They are evaluating whether the decision can withstand:

- audit,
- regulatory review,
- investor scrutiny,
- and post-resolution litigation.

Every document either strengthens that record—or weakens it.

Anything that does neither is friction.

Where Buyers Misread This Stage

Buyers often assume that more information, more dialogue, or more enthusiasm improves approval odds.

In reality, excess data increases review time, creates internal disagreement, and multiplies veto points.

Ongoing engagement is often mistaken for progress.
Repeated clarification requests usually signal unresolved internal doubt—not momentum.

Silence is not rejection.
Activity without escalation is not approval.

What Actually Happens After You Submit

A typical internal review follows this sequence:

- Servicer or special assets assembles the file
- Gaps or inconsistencies are flagged
- Internal valuation benchmarks are compared
- Foreclosure and hold alternatives are modeled
- Loss severity is stress-tested
- Legal and policy constraints are checked
- Approval authority is confirmed
- Questions are routed back down

Each loop adds time.
Each revision slightly erodes confidence.

Packages that move forward do so because they:

- anticipate objections,
- minimize revision cycles,
- and make approval feel safer than delay.

The Internal Approval Stack (You Must Survive All of It)

Your package will pass through:

- **Workout / Special Assets Officer**
- **Asset Manager / Special Servicer**
- **Credit Committee / Approval Authority**
- **Legal / Compliance**
- **Accounting / Regulatory Review**

Each layer asks a different question:

- Is the impairment real?
- Is the value defensible?
- Is the buyer credible?
- Is the process clean?
- Can we explain this later?

Your package **must answer all five**—without argument, emotion, or narrative drift.

Package Philosophy (Non-Negotiable)

A short sale package exists for one purpose:
to justify loss while reducing future risk.

It is not a pitch.
It is not a pro forma.
It is not a sympathy narrative.

If a document does not:

- reduce uncertainty,
- support impairment defensibility, or
- increase certainty of close,
- it does not belong in the file.

The Two Legitimate Package Types (Know Which You're Building)

There are always two package archetypes.

Borrower-Driven Package

Used when:

- borrower is cooperative,
- guaranty exposure exists,
- lender wants borrower participation.

Includes:

- inability-to-cure proof,
- borrower financial disclosure,
- guarantor exposure context.

Buyer-Driven Package

Used when:

- borrower is passive, frozen, or irrelevant,
- lender trusts buyer more than sponsor,
- value and execution certainty drive approval.

Focuses on:

- as-is value,
- foreclosure comparison,
- clean execution.

Confusing these two kills deals. Incomplete borrower data delays escalation and weakens servicer advocacy.

Mandatory Package Components (Non-Negotiable)

1. Executive Summary (1–2 Pages Max)

This is the most important document.

It must clearly state:

- loan status and impairment,
- why refinance or cure is impossible,
- why foreclosure is inferior,
- why the price reflects market reality,
- why the buyer will close.

If this memo fails, nothing else matters.

2. Property Overview (As-Is Reality Only)

Include:

- asset description,
- current occupancy (physical vs. economic),
- lease expiration profile,
- deferred maintenance summary,
- CapEx required to stabilize.

Exclude:

- blue-sky upside,
- future rent growth,
- "once stabilized" language.

This is about today, not hope.

3. Financial Documentation (Must Reconcile)

Required:

- trailing 12-month P&L (minimum),
- trailing 24-month P&L (preferred),
- current rent roll,
- delinquency report,
- CAM reconciliation (if applicable).

Numbers must tie.

Inconsistencies = silent rejection.

4. Proof of Inability to Cure (Critical)

Acceptable evidence includes:

- failed refinance term sheets,
- appraisals or BOVs below loan balance,
- sponsor liquidity shortfall,
- capital call failure,
- interest-rate cap costs,
- DSCR projections showing no recovery.

This must demonstrate **economic impossibility**, not inconvenience.

5. As-Is Valuation Support

Include:

- distressed BOV,
- recent distressed comps,
- cost-to-cure analysis,
- deferred maintenance estimates,
- lease rollover risk modeling.

The goal is not to argue price.

The goal is to make alternative outcomes less defensible.

6. Buyer Offer & Structure

Include:

- LOI or draft PSA,
- clean purchase price,
- earnest money terms,
- closing timeline,
- financing structure (or all-cash),
- explicit no-retrade statement.

The offer should feel boring and inevitable.

7. Buyer Credibility Proof

Must include:

- current proof of funds,
- entity structure,

- operator background or track record,
- advisors (legal, PM, GC),
- execution philosophy.

Lenders approve buyers—not just numbers.

Data Room Structure (Signal Competence)

Recommended folder structure:

1. Executive Summary
2. Loan Information
3. Financials
4. Leases & Rent Roll
5. Physical Condition / CapEx
6. Environmental
7. Valuation Support
8. Buyer Offer & POF
9. Legal / Title (if available)

Messy data rooms signal messy execution.

Submission Strategy (Control Matters)

When to Submit

Submit only when all of the following are true:

- impairment narrative is aligned,
- borrower cooperation is secured or irrelevant,
- buyer capital is verified,
- valuation support is defensible,
- and no material facts remain undisclosed.

If any item is unresolved, do not submit.

Incomplete files reset internal clocks and weaken sponsorship.

How to Submit

- single point of contact,

- single cover memo,
- no piecemeal emails,
- no "we'll send more later."

You want the reviewer to say:

> "This file is clean."

What Happens After Submission

One of three things occurs:

1. **Active Review**
   Questions, clarifications, escalation.
2. **Soft Stall**
   Silence, deprioritization, loss of sponsorship.
3. **Rejection by Inertia**
   No formal "no"—just no progress.

Your job is to prevent **#2 and #3**.

Common Failure Modes (Where Deals Die)

- inconsistent financials,
- upside-driven narratives,
- weak inability-to-cure proof,
- buyer credibility gaps,
- late environmental disclosures,
- retrade language (explicit or implied).

Once credibility is damaged, it is rarely restored.

What "Done" Looks Like

When this chapter is executed correctly:

- the file stops circulating,
- document requests slow,
- internal questions narrow,
- and conversations shift from "why" to "how."

The lender no longer asks for justification.

They begin discussing conditions, timelines, and execution.

That shift—not formal approval—is the sign the deal is alive.

Chapter 6: Buyer Strategy & Offer Control

Why Certainty Beats Price—Every Time

Primary Perspective: Buyer / Resolution Operator
Secondary Perspective: Lender
Reader Objective: Understand how certainty of close is engineered, why it consistently outweighs price in distressed approvals, and how disciplined buyers are selected over higher bidders.

Orientation: Why This Chapter Exists

By the time a short sale reaches buyer selection, the lender is no longer choosing price.
They are choosing execution risk.

This chapter exists to explain how certainty of close is engineered—and why buyers who understand this are selected repeatedly over higher bidders.

In distressed resolution, price attracts review.
Certainty earns approval.

The Buyer's Mental Model

A disciplined buyer does not approach a short sale as a negotiation.

They approach it as a risk-transfer exercise.

The operative questions are not about leverage or advantage.
They are about exposure:

- What outcome creates regret for the decision-maker?
- What failure is unacceptable?
- What uncertainty must be eliminated before it is raised?

From this perspective, the offer is not persuasion.

It is proof that risk has already been absorbed.

How Lenders Actually Compare Buyers (The Uncomfortable Truth)

Lenders do not compare buyers by price, projections, or confidence.

They compare buyers by asking one question:

> "Which buyer is least likely to create regret after approval?"

Everything that follows in this chapter exists to answer that question.

The Buyer Selection Funnel (What You're Really Competing Against)

Every short sale effectively runs this funnel:

1. Expressions of interest
2. Buyers with proof of funds
3. Buyers who submit complete packages
4. Buyers who don't retrade
5. Buyers who survive diligence
6. Buyer the lender trusts

Most buyers self-destruct at steps **3 through 5**.

Your strategy is not to "win" the funnel.
It is to enter only when you already belong at the bottom of it.

What "Certainty of Close" Actually Means

Certainty is not confidence or intent.

Certainty exists only when all required failure points have been neutralized in advance.

A buyer is considered "certain" only when all five conditions below are demonstrably true.
If any one is missing, certainty does not exist—regardless of price.

1. **Capital Availability**

Funds are present—not promised, not pending.

2. **Decision Authority**
   No investment committee lag, no partner veto risk.
3. **Timeline Realism**
   No fantasy closes. Milestones reflect reality.
4. **Risk Acceptance**
   Known risks are already priced—not deferred.
5. **Non-Retrade Culture**
   Proven through behavior, not language.

If any one is missing, certainty collapses.

Proof of Funds (The Silent Gatekeeper)

What Counts as Real Proof

Acceptable:

- current bank or custodian statements (redacted),
- equity partner confirmation letters,
- balance sheet + liquidity summary.

Unacceptable:

- screenshots,
- "investor interest,"
- unsecured LOCs,
- vague family office letters.

If proof of funds introduces questions instead of closing them, buyer credibility collapses immediately.

How Much Is Enough?

Proof of funds must cover:

- purchase price,
- closing costs,
- initial carry and CapEx buffer.

Not just the contract price.

Offer Construction: Writing an Approachable LOI

Price Philosophy

Your price should:

- be defensible, not aggressive,
- align with the as-is value narrative,
- already include known risks,
- require no renegotiation to survive diligence.

A winning price feels deliberate—not opportunistic.

Key LOI Elements Lenders Actually Care About

Your LOI should clearly state:

- purchase price (clean, round),
- meaningful earnest money,
- realistic closing timeline (60–120 days),
- financing structure (or none),
- "as-is, where-is" language,
- limited contingencies,
- explicit no-retrade commitment.

That last item matters more than price.

The No-Retrade Doctrine (Non-Negotiable)

A buyer who requires retrade flexibility is not resolution-grade.

Retrades force re-approval, invite backups, and signal execution weakness. Once a retrade occurs, buyer replaceability becomes immediate.

Legitimate vs Illegitimate Retrades

Legitimate:

- undisclosed environmental contamination,
- material title defects,
- fraud or misrepresentation.

Illegitimate:

- market softened,
- leasing slower than expected,
- CapEx higher than modeled,
- interest rates changed.

Those risks should already be priced.

How You Signal No-Retrade Credibility

You signal it by:

- conservative pricing,
- escrow holdbacks instead of price cuts,
- accepting defined risks up front,
- putting real money at risk early.

Words do not signal certainty.

Actions do.

Backup Buyers (Why You Should Encourage Them)

Lenders insist on backups because they:

- reduce execution risk,
- preserve momentum,
- discipline the primary buyer.

Resisting backups raises concern.

Strategic Posture

- Encourage one backup.
- Do not fight it.
- Stay responsive and clean.

Confidence is not exclusivity.

It is tolerance for replaceability.

Earnest Money & Escrow Structure

Earnest Money Expectations

- meaningful enough to matter,
- goes hard after defined milestones,
- released incrementally.

Lenders watch how you risk capital.

Holdbacks vs Price Cuts

When issues arise:

- use escrow holdbacks,
- define scope and release triggers,
- avoid headline price changes.

This preserves committee momentum.

Timing Strategy (The Hidden Lever)

Speed is relative.

Too fast feels reckless.

Too slow feels weak.

Optimal posture:

- calm urgency,
- predictable milestones,
- zero surprises.

Common Timing Traps

- overpromising close dates,
- underestimating diligence,
- waiting on third parties,
- letting attorneys control pace.

Pace is an execution responsibility.

If counsel controls timing, certainty erodes.

Buyer Failure Modes (Where Ego Kills Deals)

- inflating price to "win,"
- weak proof of funds,
- over-lawyering LOIs,
- arguing instead of aligning,
- reacting emotionally to delays,
- trying to outsmart servicers.

Short sales punish ego.

What "Done" Looks Like

When executed correctly:

- the lender stops comparing buyers,
- internal references shift to "our buyer,"
- and discussions focus on approvals, consents, and sequencing.

At that point, price is no longer being evaluated.
Execution is.

When a lender says, "Let's work through the process,"
selection has already occurred.

Chapter 7: Stakeholder Alignment & Intercreditor Reality

Why Approved Deals Still Die

Primary Perspective: Resolution Operator
Secondary Perspectives: Lender, Borrower / Guarantor
Reader Objective: Understand consent hierarchies, veto points, and why unresolved stakeholders derail otherwise approved transactions.

Orientation: Why This Chapter Exists

Many short sales fail *after* approval.

Not because:

- price changes,
- diligence uncovers something fatal,
- or the lender reverses course.

They fail because someone with veto power was ignored, underestimated, or addressed too late.

This chapter exists to explain a core truth:

Approval is conditional. Clearance is final.

Resolution is not about agreement.

It is about removing every party capable of stopping the transaction.

The Resolution Operator's Reality

From a resolution operator's perspective, a short sale is not a buyer–seller transaction.

It is a hierarchy of consent.

Every party above the equity stack holds some form of control:

- senior lenders,

- mezz lenders,
- preferred equity,
- junior liens,
- guarantors,
- tax authorities,
- partners with consent rights.

The job is not to negotiate with everyone.

The job is to:

- identify every veto point,
- understand its leverage,
- and deliberately choose one outcome:
- obtain consent,
- neutralize influence, or
- remove legal relevance.

Ignoring a stakeholder does not reduce their power.

It only delays when it will be exercised.

Common Misreads That Kill Deals

Buyers Misread Approval as Finality

Buyers often assume:

- approval equals certainty,
- silence equals consent,
- unresolved issues can be handled "in escrow."

None of this is true.

Approval without clearance is provisional—and reversible.

Borrowers Misread Cooperation as Protection

Borrowers often believe:

- cooperation ensures goodwill,
- junior parties will fall in line,

- guaranty issues can wait.

As pressure increases, incentives shift.

Unresolved exposure changes behavior.

How Deals Actually Die (The Quiet Version)

A common failure sequence:

- senior lender issues conditional approval
- buyer proceeds confidently
- junior lienholder surfaces late
- guarantor counsel raises objections
- tax exposure becomes visible
- one party refuses consent
- timelines slip
- confidence erodes
- approval expires or is withdrawn

No one "kills" the deal.

Risk accumulates until finishing feels irresponsible.

Professionals surface these issues **before** momentum builds—not after.

Failure Modes vs. Success Path

Failure Modes

- assuming junior liens are immaterial
- treating guarantors as passive
- discovering consent rights late
- hoping small stakeholders capitulate
- relying on informal assurances

These deals fail late—and expensively.

Success Path

- capital stack mapped exhaustively at entry

- all consent rights identified early
- leverage assessed per stakeholder
- resolution paths defined before approval
- contingencies structured intentionally

Successful deals feel uneventful because conflict was removed in advance.

Practical Rules (Non-Negotiable)

- If a party can block closing, they must be addressed early.
- If consent is assumed instead of secured, expect delay.
- If guaranty exposure is unresolved, cooperation will erode.
- If junior interests are ignored, they will surface at the worst moment.

Certainty of closing is determined by clearance— not optimism, pricing, or intent.

The Capital Stack *Is* the Deal

A short sale is not a real estate problem.
It is a capital stack problem.

Typical CRE Stack (Top to Bottom)

1. Senior mortgage lender
2. Mezzanine debt
3. Preferred equity
4. Common equity
5. Judgment creditors
6. Mechanics liens
7. Tax liens (federal, state, local)
8. UCC filings (personal property)

Any party with a recorded or contractual claim above equity must:

- consent,
- be paid,
- or be rendered legally incapable of stopping the transaction before closing is scheduled.

There is no passive clearance in commercial short sales.

Identify Every Veto Holder (Mandatory)

Veto Power Is Legal, Not Economic

Veto power comes from:

- recorded liens,
- contractual consent rights,
- intercreditor agreements,
- bankruptcy leverage,
- litigation threat.

A $50,000 lien can kill a $10MM deal.

Required Tool: Creditor & Consent Matrix

You must build a matrix with:

- party name
- claim type
- recorded position
- estimated payoff
- consent required (yes/no)
- approval authority
- negotiation leverage
- risk rating (low / medium / high)

If this document does not exist, you are guessing—and guessing kills approvals late.

Senior Lender Reality (The Gatekeeper)

What Senior Lenders Care About

- loss severity
- timeline certainty

- regulatory defensibility
- zero post-close litigation

They will not close if junior issues remain unresolved.

Typical Conditions Precedent

- all junior liens released
- settlement agreement executed
- deficiency waiver finalized
- borrower cooperation documented
- clean title commitment

The senior lender controls when the deal can close.

Junior Creditors (The #1 Late-Stage Failure Point)

The Reality

Junior creditors are rarely rational.

They are often:

- already impaired,
- out of the money,
- using consent as leverage.

Your Four Tools

1. **Token Payoff**
   Enough to allow face-saving.
2. **Release Without Payoff**
   Common when foreclosure wipes them anyway.
3. **Global Settlement**
   Wrapped into borrower deficiency resolution.
4. **Judicial Neutralization**
   Foreclosure or bankruptcy leverage.

You must select the tool **early**.

What Not to Do

- ignore juniors
- assume they'll disappear
- wait until escrow
- let the borrower handle it alone

This is the most common avoidable late-stage failure in the entire lifecycle.

CMBS & Securitized Loans (Different Physics)

Why CMBS Is Harder

- governed by PSA language
- REMIC tax constraints
- multiple committees
- zero discretion culture

There is no relationship leverage.

CMBS Approval Reality

Expect:

- formal valuation review
- NPV testing
- rigid timelines
- no process flexibility

Your leverage is certainty and cleanliness, not persuasion.

CMBS Kill Conditions

- retrades
- late environmental issues
- timing slippage
- unclear title
- borrower bankruptcy threats

Zero tolerance environment.

Tax Authorities (Silent but Lethal)

Property Taxes

- often senior
- must be current or resolved

IRS Liens

- attach to proceeds
- require formal release
- move slowly

Always identify early.

Borrower & Guarantor Alignment

Borrower Cooperation Is Not Optional—and Not Durable Without Resolution

Without it:

- estoppels fail
- access collapses
- litigation risk rises
- Borrowers cooperate when:
- deficiency exposure is addressed
- timeline is finite
- communication is respectful

Guaranty & Bad-Boy Exposure

This is often the borrower's only real motivation.

If unresolved:

- quiet sabotage begins
- counsel slows everything
- bankruptcy threats appear

Resolve this explicitly.

Settlement Architecture (Where Precision Matters)

Settlement Agreements Must Cover

- loan payoff
- lien releases
- deficiency waivers
- mutual releases
- confidentiality
- non-disparagement

This is not boilerplate.

This is risk allocation.

One Settlement or Many?

Whenever possible:

- one global settlement
- no fragmented releases
- no staggered closings

Fragmentation increases execution risk.

Timing & Sequencing (Order Is Everything)

Correct Sequence

1. Senior lender approval
2. Junior creditor negotiations
3. Borrower / guarantor settlement
4. Title clearance
5. Closing documentation

Reversing steps causes collapse—or forces re-approval.

Failure Modes (All Preventable)

Deals die when:

- junior liens surface late
- IRS timing is underestimated
- borrower counsel adds demands
- CMBS committees reset terms
- title exceptions remain
- settlement language is vague

None of these are surprises.

All are process failures.

What "Done" Looks Like

When executed correctly:

- every creditor has consented, been paid, or neutralized
- title is clean
- settlement agreements are drafted
- no hidden veto holders remain
- lender greenlights closing

At this point, the deal is structurally closable.

All stakeholders above equity have either:

a) consented,
b) been paid, or
c) been rendered legally irrelevant.

That is resolution—not agreement, not approval, and not intent.

Chapter 8: Due Diligence Without Sabotage

The Real Estate Track That Must Not Kill the Resolution

Primary Perspective: Buyer / Resolution Operator
Secondary Perspective: Lender
Reader Objective: Learn how to conduct due diligence that confirms assumptions without resetting lender risk perception, triggering retrades, or collapsing approvals.

Orientation: Why This Chapter Exists

Most buyers believe due diligence exists to discover problems.

In distressed resolution, due diligence exists to avoid introducing new risk.

This chapter exists because a significant number of approved short sales fail after approval—not because diligence uncovers fatal issues, but because it is conducted in a way that:

- reintroduces uncertainty,
- resets lender risk perception,
- or signals execution fragility.

In a short sale, diligence does not just protect the buyer.
It actively determines whether lender confidence survives to closing.

The Core Rule (Memorize This)

If a diligence finding does not change your willingness to close, it must not change the lender's perception of the deal.

Violating this rule is how approved deals lose approval without warning.

The Resolution Operator's Mindset

From a resolution operator's perspective, diligence has one primary purpose:

Confirm assumptions without altering the lender's internal risk posture.

That requires a fundamentally different approach than traditional acquisitions.

The disciplined buyer asks:

- Which assumptions are already embedded in lender approval?
- What findings would actually change price or structure?
- Which discoveries must be resolved quietly versus escalated?
- What information would force re-review?

Not every risk needs to be surfaced.

Every surfaced risk forces re-evaluation.

Diligence must be selective, intentional, and aligned with the approval narrative.

Where Buyers and Lenders Misread Diligence

Buyers Misread Diligence as Leverage

Many buyers assume:

- diligence creates renegotiation rights,
- surprises create bargaining power,
- lenders expect flexibility post-approval.

In distressed resolution, retrades are interpreted execution failure—not prudence or diligence.

Lenders Misread Diligence Noise as Instability

Lenders interpret:

- frequent new questions,
- rotating consultants,
- shifting assumptions,
- as signals the buyer may not close.

Once that doubt forms, approvals weaken quietly and timelines stop compressing..

How Deals Actually Die During Diligence

A typical failure sequence:

- buyer secures approval
- full-scope diligence launches
- minor issues are elevated
- consultants frame worst-case scenarios
- questions are routed back to the lender
- internal risk perception resets
- timelines extend
- confidence erodes
- approval expires or is withdrawn

No one disputes the findings.

They simply make finishing feel less defensible.

Professionals treat diligence as confirmation, not exploration.

Failure Modes vs. Success Path

Failure Modes

- using diligence to reset economics
- introducing new third-party opinions late
- escalating non-fatal issues
- letting consultants control risk framing
- failing to distinguish deal-killers from management issues

These actions increase perceived execution risk.

Success Path

- diligence scoped tightly to known assumptions
- internal thresholds for retrade decisions set in advance
- quiet resolution of manageable issues
- escalation only when structurally necessary
- consistent messaging throughout

Successful diligence is nearly invisible to the lender because it confirms what was already approved.

Practical Rules (Non-Negotiable)

- If diligence does not change your close decision, it must not change lender perception.
- If a retrade depends on diligence, approval probability collapses immediately.
- If consultants introduce uncertainty, they must be managed—not indulged.
- If new risks surface late, expect re-review.
- The goal of diligence is certainty, not perfection.

Two Tracks, One Clock (Critical Concept)

Every short sale runs on two parallel tracks:

1. **Loan Resolution Track**
   (approvals, consents, settlements)
2. **Real Estate Track**
   (physical, legal, operational diligence)

They must move together.

If real-estate diligence introduces uncertainty after lender confidence has stabilized, deals die.

Due Diligence Philosophy (This Is Different)

Traditional Deals Use DD To:

- find upside,
- justify price cuts,
- renegotiate terms.

Short Sales Use DD To:

- confirm no hidden landmines,

- validate risks already priced,
- support closing—not reset it.

Mindset shift:

Anything you reasonably expect to find should already be priced in.

Physical Due Diligence: What Actually Matters

Required Reviews

- Property Condition Assessment (PCA)
- roof systems
- HVAC (age, redundancy, remaining life)
- life-safety systems
- ADA compliance
- parking and paving
- deferred maintenance inventory

True Deal-Killers

- structural failure
- uninsurable conditions
- incurable life-safety violations
- deferred CapEx exceeding the explicit pricing buffer

Not Deal-Killers

- old roofs
- end-of-life HVAC
- cosmetic deterioration
- outdated finishes

Those are management issues—not surprises.

Environmental Due Diligence (Zero-Tolerance Zone)

Environmental issues are the fastest way to lose lender confidence.

Unidentified environmental conditions discovered after approval are automatic grounds for termination.

Phase I ESA (Mandatory)

Purpose:

- identify RECs
- establish liability protection
- satisfy lender requirements

Phase II Triggers

- industrial history
- dry cleaners
- gas stations
- USTs
- heavy manufacturing
- known contamination

Late discovery is often a hard stop.

Environmental Risk Handling

- identify early
- quantify costs
- structure escrow holdbacks if feasible
- **never surprise the lender**

Title & Survey (Hidden Veto Layer)

Title Review Focus

- unresolved liens
- easements affecting use
- access defects
- unreleased UCCs
- judgments

Late title defects derail closings and force re-approval.

ALTA Survey Review

Confirm:

- legal access
- setbacks
- parking compliance
- encroachments
- zoning conformity

Zoning, Use, and Entitlements

Distressed assets often operate on thin legal margins.

Confirm:

- zoning compliance
- legal non-conforming status
- continued use rights
- re-tenanting limits
- expansion constraints

Never assume "grandfathered" equals safe.

Lease & Tenant Forensics (NOI Is the Asset)

Lease Audit (Mandatory)

Reconcile:

- leases vs rent roll
- billed vs collected rent
- CAM recoveries
- TI / LC exposure
- renewal and termination rights
- co-tenancy clauses

Phantom NOI kills underwriting credibility.

Estoppels & SNDAs

Used to:

- confirm obligations
- protect buyer and lender
- prevent post-close disputes

Handle carefully to avoid tenant panic.

Insurance & Insurability (Often Missed)

Insurability is a closing condition.

Confirm:

- property can be insured
- premiums are feasible
- deductibles are manageable
- exclusions don't break economics

Uninsurable properties cannot close, regardless of price.

Timing & Sequencing

When to Start Diligence

Begin diligence:

- **after** lender signals approval direction
- **before** final committee sign-off

Too early wastes money.

Too late invites surprises.

Kill Screen Discipline

If diligence reveals a true deal-killer:

- walk early
- walk quietly
- walk professionally

Walking early preserves credibility with lenders and servicers.

Failure Modes (All Preventable)

Deals die when:

- buyers hunt for retrades
- environmental issues surface late
- title defects are ignored
- tenants are spooked
- insurability is assumed
- attorneys control timelines instead of the resolution operator

Short sales punish sloppy diligence.

What "Done" Looks Like

When executed correctly:

- no unknown fatal risks remain
- known issues are priced or structured
- lender confidence is preserved
- closing path is clean
- no justification for retrade exists

At this point, execution risk collapses or becomes immediately visible.
The deal either closes—or dies cleanly—without reputational damage.

Chapter 9: Negotiation Playbook

Leverage Without Ego, Outcomes Without Damage

Primary Perspective: Resolution Operator
Secondary Perspectives: Borrower / Guarantor, Lender
Reader Objective: Learn how to structure negotiations so closing becomes the least risky option for all parties—eliminating resistance before it hardens.

Orientation: Why This Chapter Exists

Most negotiations do not fail loudly.

They fail quietly.

Not because:

- price is unresolved,
- positions are irreconcilable,
- or leverage is insufficient.

They fail because residual resistance survives past agreement.

This chapter exists to reframe negotiation away from tactics and toward friction removal.

In distressed resolution, negotiation is not about extracting advantage—it is about making closing feel safer than delay for every party involved.

If resistance exists at closing, the deal is unlikely to survive execution—approval notwithstanding.

The Resolution Operator's Mental Model

Negotiation is not combat.
It is diagnostic and corrective.

The core questions are:

- Where is the resistance?
- What exposure or fear is driving it?

- What outcome does each party need to feel protected?
- What must be resolved for cooperation to persist through closing?

Negotiation is not a series of concessions.

It is a reallocation of risk.

Any unresolved concern—legal, financial, reputational, or emotional —will surface later as delay or resistance if ignored now.

Where Negotiations Commonly Go Wrong

Buyers Misread Negotiation as Leverage Exercise

Buyers often assume:

- pressure accelerates agreement,
- urgency creates concessions,
- firmness signals strength.

In distressed resolution, pressure usually increases defensiveness and slows progress.

Strength is demonstrated by risk absorption and control, not force.

Borrowers Misread Negotiation as Moral Reckoning

Borrowers often approach negotiation emotionally:

- seeking validation,
- resisting loss acknowledgment,
- reacting defensively to perceived judgment.

If these dynamics are dismissed, cooperation erodes—even after economics are agreed.

How Deals Actually Die in Negotiation

A common failure sequence:

- economic terms are agreed
- legal details are deferred

- guaranty exposure remains unresolved
- tax consequences are underestimated
- one party's counsel reframes risk
- resistance hardens late
- momentum stalls
- approval expires

No one reopens price.

They simply stop moving toward closing.

Professionals surface resistance early, while options still exist.

Failure Modes vs. Success Path

Failure Modes

- treating negotiation as adversarial
- deferring "minor" issues to closing
- assuming silence equals acceptance
- ignoring emotional or reputational drivers
- allowing advisors to introduce new risk framing late

These deals unravel at the finish line.

Success Path

- resistance identified early
- guaranty and deficiency issues resolved explicitly
- tax and legal consequences addressed upfront
- advisors aligned before documents circulate
- closing framed as risk elimination rather than concession

Successful negotiations feel anticlimactic.

That is not weakness.

That is professional resolution.

Practical Rules (Decision Discipline)

- If resistance is deferred, it will return at closing.
- If negotiation feels adversarial, structural alignment is missing.
- If advisors are surprised, expect delay.
- If emotional concerns are dismissed, cooperation degrades.
- Negotiation succeeds only when closing feels safer than delay.

What Negotiation Is—and Is Not

Negotiation Is

- risk allocation
- timeline control
- liability resolution
- permission engineering

Negotiation Is Not

- price discovery
- moral judgment
- sponsor punishment
- cleverness contests

If negotiation reopens value, control has already been lost.

The Only Leverage That Actually Matters

You have leverage only if you control one or more of the following:

- **Certainty of close** (capital + discipline)
- **Time** (standstill, forbearance, calendar control)
- **Alternatives** (backup buyers or foreclosure readiness)
- **Process clarity** (clean file, no surprises)
- **Reputational safety** (no litigation, no headlines)

Money alone is rarely leverage.

Buyers without visible liquidity, execution history, and retrade discipline are discounted—regardless of price.

Deficiency Waivers: The Borrower's Real Deal

Why This Matters

For borrowers and guarantors, this *is* the deal.

Without a defined deficiency path:

- cooperation degrades,
- timelines slip,
- quiet resistance and delay appear.

When Lenders Grant Waivers

Deficiency waivers are granted when:

- loss severity is defensible,
- borrower cooperation is complete,
- no fraud or bad-boy triggers exist,
- litigation risk is minimized,
- the buyer is credible.

Waivers are earned, not demanded.

How to Frame the Waiver

Never frame as mercy.

Frame as:

> "A clean exit that eliminates future litigation risk and ensures full co-operation through closing."

That language survives committee scrutiny.

Guaranty & Bad-Boy Carveout Releases

What Lenders Fear

- hidden fraud
- reputational exposure
- precedent risk

What Lenders Will Release

- standard payment guaranties
- completion guaranties
- non-recourse carveouts (absent misconduct)

What Rarely Gets Released

- proven fraud
- environmental misconduct
- criminal acts

Overreaching poisons trust.

Standstill & Forbearance as Tools

Why They Matter

Standstills:

- stop foreclosure momentum
- buy time for alignment
- signal lender openness
- reduce borrower panic

How to Use Them Properly

They must be:

- time-bound
- milestone-driven

- conditioned on cooperation

Standstills are bridges to closing, not parking lots.

Holdbacks vs. Price Reductions

Why Price Cuts Are Dangerous

- require formal re-approval
- reset committees
- invite retrades
- signal instability

When Holdbacks Work Better

Use escrow holdbacks for:

- defined CapEx
- environmental monitoring
- tenant disputes
- unresolved punch-list items

Holdbacks preserve approval while managing risk.

Timeline Control: The Quiet Lever

Delays increase:

- legal costs
- carry costs
- uncertainty
- committee fatigue

Your job is to make delay structurally unattractive.

How to Control Time

- define milestones clearly
- tie concessions to speed
- maintain quiet backups

- escalate professionally, not emotionally

Time is leverage when managed deliberately.

Negotiating with CMBS / Special Servicers

Reality Check

There is:

- no discretion
- no sympathy
- no creativity

Only:

- compliance
- process
- certainty

CMBS Leverage Points

- flawless documentation
- zero retrades
- disciplined timelines
- no surprises

CMBS negotiations are decided before they begin.

What Never to Say

Avoid:

- "This is the best we can do"
- "The market changed"
- "We need to revisit price"
- "Our investors are nervous"
- "We found additional issues"

These statements reset review and reopen risk assessment.

Failure Modes (Predictable and Preventable)

Deals die when:

- negotiation becomes emotional
- borrower counsel grandstands
- buyer pushes too hard
- lender feels cornered
- timelines drift
- waivers are treated casually

Short sales reward disciplined restraint.

What "Done" Looks Like

When executed correctly:

- final economic terms are fixed
- deficiency waiver language is settled
- guaranty releases are defined
- standstill converts cleanly into closing
- no material negotiation items remain

At this point, nothing substantive is left that should be debated.

The deal either closes—or fails cleanly—without drama.

Chapter 10: Legal & Tax Coordination

Where Deals Survive Scrutiny—or Unravel

Primary Perspective: Borrower / Resolution Operator
Secondary Perspective: Lender
Reader Objective: Understand how legal structure, guaranty exposure, and tax consequences shape borrower behavior—and why unresolved consequences kill deals late.

Orientation: Why This Chapter Exists

Many short sales die after economics are settled.

Not because:

- parties disagree,
- approvals are revoked,
- or diligence uncovers fatal flaws.

They die because legal and tax consequences are surfaced too late—or not at all.

This chapter exists to explain why:

- deals that "make sense" unravel,
- borrower cooperation collapses suddenly,
- and advisors become inadvertent deal-killers.

In distressed resolution, ignorance of consequences is not neutrality.
It is deferred resistance that surfaces at closing.

The Borrower's Reality (This Is Existential)

From the borrower's perspective, **legal and tax outcomes are not technical details.**

They determine:

- personal liability,

- future creditworthiness,
- litigation exposure,
- and tax bills with no liquidity to pay them.

Borrowers will agree to economics they do not fully understand—until counsel explains the consequences.

That moment reorders incentives instantly.

The Resolution Operator's Responsibility

From the resolution operator's perspective, none of this is surprising.

The critical questions are:

- What legal exposure remains post-close?
- What tax consequences are triggered?
- When will the borrower discover them?
- Who will explain them—and in what frame?

If these answers emerge after approval, cooperation is already at risk.

Where Deals Go Wrong

Buyers Misread Silence as Acceptance

Buyers often assume:

- agreement implies understanding,
- legal language is boilerplate,
- tax issues are "the borrower's problem."

They are not.

When consequences become clear, borrower behavior changes immediately.

Lenders Misread Legal Closure as Finality

Lenders sometimes assume:

- settlement language resolves exposure,
- releases are sufficient,
- cooperation is durable.

Unresolved guaranty or tax exposure can still halt closing—even after approval.

How Legal & Tax Issues Kill Deals (Quietly)

A typical failure sequence:

- economics agreed
- approval issued
- documents circulate
- borrower counsel reviews consequences
- CODI exposure becomes visible
- guaranty language tightens
- advisors recommend delay, restructuring, or renegotiation
- borrower resists closing
- momentum collapses

No one disputes price.

They dispute consequences.

Professionals surface consequences early, explain them clearly, and resolve them explicitly.

Failure Modes vs. Success Path

Failure Modes

- treating legal language as mere formality
- deferring tax analysis until documents circulate
- allowing advisors to introduce surprises late
- assuming borrower risk tolerance
- failing to coordinate messaging

These deals unravel *after* appearing "done."

Success Path

- legal and tax implications surfaced early
- borrower counsel engaged before approvals

- deficiency and release language addressed explicitly
- tax consequences explained plainly
- advisors aligned around closing rather than delay

Successful deals feel understood, not merely agreed.

Practical Rules (Hard Discipline)

- If legal exposure is unclear, resistance will surface later.
- If tax consequences are discovered late, expect delay.
- If borrower advisors are surprised, the deal is at risk.
- If releases are incomplete, cooperation degrades.

Clarity preserves momentum.
Ambiguity destroys it.

The Cardinal Rule

Legal and tax outcomes must align with deal economics before documents are drafted.

If attorneys or CPAs discover previously unaddressed material exposure after pricing and approval:

- negotiations reopen,
- committees reset,
- trust erodes,
- closings slip—or die.

This chapter exists to prevent that.

Deficiency Exposure (The Real Legal Risk)

What a Deficiency Is

A deficiency equals:

- outstanding loan balance (plus costs)
- minus net sale proceeds.

In many jurisdictions, this is legally collectible against the borrower and/or guarantors.

Recourse vs. "Non-Recourse" (With Reality)

Even "non-recourse" loans commonly include:

- bad-boy carveouts,
- completion guaranties,
- environmental indemnities,
- fraud and misrepresentation clauses.

Assume exposure exists until counsel proves otherwise.

Why Deficiency Must Be Resolved Early

If deficiency exposure remains unresolved:

- borrower cooperation erodes,
- counsel escalates,
- bankruptcy threats emerge,
- closing risk spikes abruptly.

Deficiency resolution is not optional.

It is a deal condition.

Deficiency Waivers & Releases (Mechanics Matter)

What Lenders Will Consider

- full deficiency waivers
- conditional waivers upon closing
- covenant-not-to-sue structures
- mutual releases

What Lenders Will Not Agree To

- releases that obscure fraud
- language limiting regulatory authority
- vague carveout provisions

Drafting Discipline

Deficiency language must:

- be explicit,
- survive assignment,
- bind successors,
- be properly recorded or referenced.

Vague releases are future litigation.

CODI – Cancellation of Debt Income (The Tax Landmine)

What CODI Is

Forgiven debt is treated as taxable income unless an exception applies.

This is often the borrower's largest remaining unresolved risk.

Why CODI Kills Deals

Deals die when:

- CODI is discovered late,
- CPAs panic,
- sellers demand price changes or structure revisions,
- closings pause "for tax review."

All of this is avoidable.

Late CODI discovery causes borrower resistance and late-stage delay.

Common CODI Exceptions (Not Automatic)

- insolvency exception
- bankruptcy exception
- qualified real property business indebtedness (QRPBI)
- partnership-level allocations

Each requires documentation. None apply by default.

Insolvency Exception (Often Misunderstood)

Definition:

> Liabilities exceed fair market value of assets immediately before discharge.

Key realities:

- balance-sheet based
- snapshot-specific
- documentation-driven

If insolvency is not documented before debt discharge, the exception may fail.

Partnership & Entity-Level Tax Issues

Partnership Allocations

In partnerships:

- CODI flows to partners,
- allocations depend on operating agreements,
- disagreements can surface abruptly and destructively.

This kills deals late.

Entity Cleanliness

Confirm early:

- authority to sell
- valid resolutions
- no undisclosed disputes
- no pending dissolution or litigation

Corporate chaos is closing poison in distressed resolutions.

State & Local Tax Traps

Confirm early:

- transfer taxes

- documentary stamp taxes
- withholding requirements (e.g., FIRPTA)
- unpaid state or local taxes

Escrow is too late.

Attorney & CPA Coordination (Control Point)

The Hidden Risk

Advisors are trained to:

- identify risk,
- reduce liability,
- slow down.

They are not trained to close distressed resolutions.

How to Manage Advisors

You must:

- brief advisors early,
- define deal parameters,
- establish non-negotiables,
- align them to the resolution objective.

Unmanaged advisors reopen issues already settled.

Required Artifacts (Before Advancing)

Before moving to closing, you must have:

- written deficiency waiver terms
- high-level borrower tax impact analysis
- CPA acknowledgment of CODI path
- settlement agreement framework
- entity authority documentation
- legal sign-off on structure

If any are missing, do not advance toward closing.

Failure Modes (All Preventable)

Deals unravel when:

- CODI surfaces late
- deficiency language is vague
- borrower counsel escalates
- partner disputes emerge
- tax advisors demand restructuring
- timelines pause "pending review"

None of these are surprises.

All are process failures.

What "Done" Looks Like

When executed correctly:

- legal exposure is contained
- tax consequences are understood (even if painful)
- borrower cooperation holds
- lender confidence remains intact
- no late-stage surprises exist

At this point, the deal is legally and fiscally survivable.

Not optimized.

Not painless.

But executable—and final.

Chapter 11: Closing & Lien Release

Execution Without Drama

Primary Perspective: Lender / Title / Escrow
Secondary Perspective: Buyer
Reader Objective: Understand why approved short sales fail at closing—and how disciplined execution converts approval into recorded, permanent resolution.

Orientation: Why This Chapter Exists

Many short sales receive full approval and still fail to close.

Not because:

- parties disagree,
- retrades occur,
- or bad faith emerges.

They fail because execution breaks down at the moment risk becomes permanent.

This chapter exists to explain why:

- approvals expire,
- lien releases lag,
- documents stall,
- and momentum collapses at the finish line.

Closing is not clerical.
It is the final and irreversible risk event.

The Closing Mindset (Critical Shift)

By the time closing begins:

- negotiation is over,
- discovery is over,

- flexibility is gone.

The only remaining objective is flawless execution.

If anyone attempts to reopen economics, structure, or exposure at this stage, the correct response is simple:

"That issue was addressed earlier. We are now in execution."

Deals that reopen here almost never close.

How Closing Looks from the Lender / Title / Escrow Perspective

Up until closing, lender risk has been:

- internal,
- theoretical,
- reversible.

At closing, risk becomes:

- public,
- recorded,
- permanent.

From this perspective, the dominant concerns are:

- lien extinguishment certainty,
- document accuracy,
- funds-flow integrity,
- enforceability of releases,
- post-close defensibility under audit, litigation, or regulatory review.

Any ambiguity at this stage feels dangerous—even if it was tolerated earlier.

Where Other Perspectives Misread Closing Risk

Buyers Misread Approval as Momentum

Buyers often believe:

- approval means "we're done,"

- closing is procedural,
- urgency creates flexibility.

In reality, closing dramatically increases caution.

Buyers Misread Delays as Gamesmanship

Late-stage pauses are often misinterpreted as:

- leverage plays,
- disorganization,
- bad faith.

More often, they reflect last-mile risk aversion by parties whose exposure is about to be recorded and permanent.

What Actually Happens When Closings Fail

A common failure sequence:

- approval issued
- closing scheduled optimistically
- title uncovers unresolved lien
- release language raises concern
- payoff figures change or expire
- counsel requests clarification
- documents circulate repeatedly
- approval window tightens
- confidence erodes
- deal expires

No one rejects the transaction.

They simply stop being willing to convert approval into recordation.

Failure Modes vs. Success Path

Failure Modes

- treating closing as administrative rather than risk-critical

- discovering liens late
- conditional or incomplete releases
- poor coordination between counsel and escrow
- assuming post-close cleanup is acceptable

These deals die inches from the finish line.

Success Path

- closing logistics planned during negotiation
- lien status exhaustively confirmed
- release language pre-cleared
- payoff figures locked
- funds flow rehearsed
- post-close verification defined and scheduled

Successful closings feel uneventful because risk was removed in advance.

Practical Rules (Non-Negotiable)

- If lien releases are unclear, closing will stall.
- If documents introduce new exposure, approval weakens immediately.
- If funds flow is uncertain, execution risk spikes.
- If post-close verification is skipped, residual risk remains.

Closing success depends on preparation—not urgency.

Closing Preconditions (Do Not Set a Date Until True)

Never schedule closing unless all of the following are complete or contractually locked:

- final lender approval issued
- all required consents obtained
- settlement agreement finalized in principle
- title commitments reviewed and cleared
- lien payoff figures confirmed
- deficiency waiver language agreed

- buyer funds confirmed and liquid
- escrow instructions drafted

If even one item is "still being worked," closing will slip—or fail.

The Settlement Agreement (The Spine of Closing)

This document often matters more than the deed.

It:

- documents the short payoff,
- releases borrower and guarantors (as agreed),
- resolves intercreditor claims,
- defines post-close obligations,
- prevents future litigation.

Settlement Agreement Must Explicitly Address:

- loan payoff amount
- lien releases
- deficiency waiver or covenant-not-to-sue
- mutual releases
- confidentiality
- non-disparagement
- no admission of wrongdoing
- binding successors and assigns

Ambiguity here creates future litigation.

Lien Releases (Never Assume—Always Verify)

Required Releases

- senior mortgage release or reconveyance
- junior lien releases
- judgment releases
- UCC termination statements

- tax lien releases (if applicable)

Each must be:

- executed,
- delivered,
- recorded.

Golden Rule:

If it's not recorded, it does not exist.

Emails, promises, and draft documents do not clear title.

Payoff Mechanics & Funds Flow

Funds Flow Discipline

- all funds through escrow
- disbursement strictly per written instructions
- no side payments
- no off-HUD or side arrangements

Transparency protects everyone.

Waterfall Confirmation

Before closing:

- review settlement statement line by line
- confirm every creditor payoff
- confirm escrow holdbacks
- confirm taxes and recording fees

Errors here delay recording and can collapse closings.

Borrower & Tenant Transition

Possession & Access

Confirm:

- possession timing

- keys, codes, systems
- management handoff

Tenant Notices

Prepare:

- change-of-ownership notices
- rent redirection instructions
- management contact information

Poor tenant handling can destabilize NOI immediately.

Timing & Coordination (No Surprises Allowed)

Final Closing Call

Participants:

- escrow
- title
- lender counsel
- buyer counsel
- seller counsel (if involved)

Agenda:

- document readiness
- funds confirmation
- recording order
- release execution and delivery

Same-Day Recording Priority

Ensure:

- deed records correctly
- lien releases record correctly
- settlement references are correct

Recording order matters.

Common Closing Killers (All Preventable)

Deals fail when:

- a payoff figure is wrong
- a release is missing
- a document is unsigned
- funds are delayed
- a party introduces a new condition
- advisors argue jurisdictional minutiae

None are "economic problems."

They are execution failures.

Post-Close Verification (Mandatory)

Within 24–72 hours:

- confirm deed recorded
- confirm all releases recorded
- obtain recording receipts
- archive final settlement statement
- track escrow holdbacks

Assume nothing until independently verified.

What "Done" Looks Like

When executed correctly:

- title transferred
- all liens released of record
- borrower and guarantors released (as agreed)
- funds disbursed correctly
- no remaining veto holders
- no loose ends

The deal is legally finished.

The property is conveyed.

The liens are extinguished.

No party retains a credible legal claim.

Chapter 12: Post-Close Value Creation

Basis Reset, Stabilization, and Why This Was Worth Doing

Primary Perspective: Buyer / Operator
Secondary Perspective: Lender (reputation, memory, and future access)
Reader Objective: Learn how to preserve basis advantage, stabilize correctly, and convert resolution skill into repeatable deal flow and long-term credibility.

Orientation: Why This Chapter Exists

Most people believe the short sale ends at closing.

It does not.

Closing is merely the moment when execution risk transfers from paper to reality.

This chapter exists because:

- basis advantage can be squandered quickly,
- post-close chaos erodes credibility,
- and disciplined operators convert one resolved deal into a platform.

Resolution only matters if it compounds into durable advantage.

The Post-Close Reality

From the buyer's perspective, the period immediately after closing determines whether the transaction was:

- a one-time opportunity, or
- the beginning of durable access.

The disciplined operator asks—immediately:

- Which assumptions justified this basis?
- Which risks were tolerated but not eliminated?
- What instability could undermine NOI now?

- What early actions signal competence to counterparties?

The goal is not optimization.

The goal is stability.

Early chaos erases the margin created by resolution.

Where Others Misread the Moment

Buyers Misread Basis as Forgiveness

Some buyers assume:

- low basis absorbs mistakes,
- deferred action is acceptable,
- upside should be chased immediately.

In reality, basis buys forgiveness only when discipline follows immediately.

Lenders Misread Silence as Irrelevance

Lenders and servicers may step back after closing—but they remember outcomes.

Poor post-close execution quietly damages:

- internal sponsorship,
- future access,
- credibility in distressed channels.

Reputation compounds faster—and lasts longer—than returns.

The Most Common Post-Close Failure Pattern

It looks like this:

- asset closes at attractive basis
- operational changes are delayed
- tenant issues linger
- CapEx priorities blur
- cash flow underperforms
- stabilization slips

- lender confidence erodes quietly

No one complains.

They simply stop offering access.

Failure Modes vs. Success Path

Failure Modes

- chasing upside before stability
- delaying visible fixes
- levering aggressively post-close
- ignoring early warning signals
- treating the deal as isolated

These operators win transactions—and forfeit platforms.

Success Path

- immediate operational stabilization
- conservative leverage decisions
- CapEx aligned to original assumptions
- disciplined communication
- deliberate pacing toward upside

Strong post-close execution confirms the narrative that justified approval.

Core Operating Rules (Post-Close)

- If early operations wobble, basis erodes immediately.
- If execution contradicts approval assumptions, credibility suffers.
- If lenders regret approving the deal, access closes.
- If the first 90 days are disciplined, resolution skill compounds.
- Long-term advantage comes from repeatability—not singular wins.

The Basis Reset (Your Only Free Lunch)

Your basis reset is not merely a low price.

It is:

- margin for error,
- downside protection,
- time to execute correctly.

You destroy it by:

- over-building,
- over-amenitizing,
- over-leveraging,
- over-hiring,
- over-promising.

Discipline preserves basis.

Ego burns it quickly.

The First 90 Days (Outcomes Are Largely Locked Here)

Immediate Priorities (Order Matters)

1. Stabilize Operations

- rent collection
- vendor continuity
- tenant communication

2. Secure the Asset

- insurance finalized
- life-safety cured
- deferred maintenance triaged

3. Establish Control

- property management aligned
- reporting cleaned
- CapEx governance enforced

What Not to Do

Do not:

- rebrand immediately
- announce "big plans"
- chase market rent
- launch major CapEx out of sequence

Stability first.

Optimization only after stability.

CapEx Sequencing (Where Value Is Usually Lost)

CapEx must be:

- sequential,
- ROI-gated,
- reversible when possible.

Priority Stack

- Life safety / compliance
- Asset protection
- Revenue protection
- Revenue enhancement
- Cosmetic / branding

Skipping layers destroys ROI—regardless of basis.

Leasing & Revenue Discipline

NOI is still the asset.

Post-distress leasing should emphasize:

- durable occupancy,
- credit-appropriate tenants,
- predictable cash flow.

Avoid:

- over-concessing,
- poor tenant mix,
- incompatible uses,

- excessive termination rights.

Bad leases outlive bad markets—and good intentions.

Expense Rationalization (Quiet, Durable Alpha)

Early value creation often comes from expenses:

- insurance rebids
- CAM audits
- vendor renegotiation
- utilities optimization
- tax appeals

These improvements compound quietly—and credibly.

Financing & Refinance Timing

Refinancing too early is a common mistake.

Refinance only when:

- NOI is proven, not projected
- leases have seasoning
- CapEx is largely complete
- market conditions cooperate
- underwriting aligns with reality

Liquidity is optionality—not obligation.

Exit Optionality (The Real Win)

A successful short-sale acquisition creates multiple exits:

- long-term hold
- refinance + hold
- recapitalization
- partial sale
- full disposition

The best exit is the one you are not forced to take.

The Reputation Flywheel (The Hidden Asset)

Lenders remember:

- who closed cleanly,
- who didn't retrade,
- who handled issues professionally,
- who didn't create post-close noise.

After closing:

- thank counterparties
- close the loop
- confirm clean execution
- stay visible—but not needy

This is how the next opportunity finds you.

Common Post-Close Killers

Value is destroyed when:

- CapEx overruns go unmanaged
- management underperforms
- leasing chases speed over quality
- leverage creeps
- confidence quietly turns into complacency

Distress punishes arrogance after the win.

What "Done" Looks Like

When executed correctly:

- operations are stabilized
- basis is protected
- NOI improves
- financing options multiply
- exits are optional
- lender relationships strengthen

The short sale is no longer just a transaction.
It has become a repeatable advantage.

Final Truth

Short sales don't make money.
Operators do.

And the operators who understand resolution—end-to-end—will consistently control assets others never manage to close.

Epilogue: Resolution Is a Discipline

Most people who touch distressed real estate believe they are participating in transactions.

They are not.

They are navigating systems—legal, financial, institutional, and human—engineered to resist error, embarrassment, and uncertainty. Assets rarely fail on their own. Structures fail first. And those structures resolve only when someone understands how to remove friction without introducing new exposure.

That is what this book has been about.

Not how to:

- negotiate harder
- buy cheaper
- or "win"

But how resolution actually occurs when no party can afford error.

By now, one theme should be unavoidable:

- **Distress does not resolve when leverage is applied.**
- **It resolves when certainty replaces fear.**

Lenders approve outcomes they can defend.

Borrowers cooperate when exposure is resolved.

Committees move when risk feels contained.

Deals close when no one is asked to gamble at the end.

This is not deal-making in the retail sense.

It is professional resolution.

Those who master it do not rely on luck, charm, or opportunism. They build files that survive scrutiny. They structure offers that eliminate retrade risk. They manage diligence without destabilizing confidence. They clear stakeholders before momentum forms. They close cleanly—and they are remembered for it.

That memory is the asset.

Because in distressed markets, access is not advertised.

It is granted—quietly—to operators who have proven they understand the burden that comes with resolution.

If you take nothing else from this book, take this:

- Every distressed opportunity is someone else's risk problem.
- When you do, doors open again—without being asked.
- Your job is to absorb it competently.

When you do, price becomes secondary.
When you do, resistance softens.
When you do, doors open again—without asking.

That is why the most successful operators are rarely the loudest.
They do not chase volume.
They do not celebrate discounts.
They do not confuse aggression with control.

They resolve.

And in markets where others stall, posture, or litigate—the resolvers continue closing.

Quietly.
Cleanly.
Repeatably.

That is the work.

"Now it is required that those who have been given a trust must prove faithful." — 1 Corinthians 4:2

Appendices

Appendix A – Terms & Acronyms

(Resolution-Grade Definitions for Distressed Commercial Real Estate)

Appraisal Reduction Amount (ARA)

Definition: A valuation adjustment used in CMBS to recognize impairment.

Perspective Notes:

- **Trust**: Accounting mechanism
- **Borrower**: Negative signal
- **Buyer**: Entry indicator

Why It Matters: ARA acknowledgment increases short-sale probability.

As-Is Value

Definition: The market-clearing price of a property in its current physical, legal, and operational condition, without assumptions of stabilization or future improvement.

Perspective Notes:

- **Lender**: The only defensible value in a loss scenario
- **Borrower**: Often emotionally rejected
- **Buyer**: Must be accepted before diligence begins

Why It Matters: Short sales are approved on as-is value, not pro forma value. Confusing the two kills deals.

As-Is vs As-Stabilized (Explicit Contrast Entry)

Definition: As-Is reflects current condition and risk; As-Stabilized reflects hypothetical future performance after capital, leasing, or market improvement.

Why It Matters: Most buyer–lender friction comes from unspoken substitution of stabilized assumptions into loss decisions. This definition gives you permission to shut that down cleanly.

As-Is vs As-Stabilized Value

Definition: A distinction between current market value based on existing conditions (as-is) and hypothetical future value assuming capital investment, leasing, or operational improvement (as-stabilized).

Perspective Notes:

- **Lender:** Only as-is value is defensible for loss decisions
- **Borrower:** Often conflated to resist impairment
- **Buyer:** Must accept as-is before diligence begins

Why It Matters: Substituting stabilized assumptions into loss justification is the fastest way to lose lender confidence and kill a short sale.

Bad-Boy Carveouts

Definition: Exceptions to non-recourse loan provisions that trigger personal liability upon specified borrower misconduct.

Perspective Notes:

- **Lender**: Risk containment mechanism
- **Borrower**: Primary source of anxiety
- **Buyer**: Indirectly determines cooperation

Why It Matters: Misunderstood carveouts derail deficiency negotiations late.

Basis Reset

Definition: The reduction in all-in acquisition cost achieved through debt resolution rather than market competition.

Perspective Notes:

- **Lender**: Loss realization
- **Borrower**: Exit relief
- **Buyer**: Margin for error

Why It Matters: Basis is advantage only if preserved post-close.

BOV (Broker Opinion of Value)

Definition: A non-binding valuation opinion prepared by a broker, often used to support loss justification.

Perspective Notes:

- **Lender**: Narrative support
- **Borrower**: Often contested

- **Buyer**: Pricing shield

Why It Matters: A BOV framed incorrectly increases scrutiny instead of reducing it.

Capital Stack

Definition: The hierarchy of financial claims against a property, from senior debt to equity.

Perspective Notes:

- **Lender**: Priority and recovery
- **Borrower**: Constraint field
- **Buyer**: Clearance problem

Why It Matters: Short sales fail when veto power is misunderstood.

Certainty of Close

Definition: The demonstrated ability to close a transaction without re-trade, delay, or capital failure.

Perspective Notes:

- **Lender**: Primary selection criterion
- **Borrower**: Source of confidence
- **Buyer**: Must be proven, not claimed

Why It Matters: Certainty beats price in distressed resolution.

CMBS (Commercial Mortgage-Backed Securities)

Definition: A securitized pool of commercial mortgage loans sold to bond investors.

Perspective Notes:

- **Lender / Trust**: Fiduciary obligation to bondholders
- **Borrower**: Reduced flexibility
- **Buyer**: Process rigidity risk

Why It Matters: CMBS short sales are process-driven, not relationship-driven.

CODI (Cancellation of Debt Income)

Definition: Taxable income recognized when debt is forgiven, unless an exclusion applies.

Perspective Notes:

- **Lender**: Non-issue

- **Borrower**: Often deal-breaking
- **Buyer**: Timing risk

Why It Matters: *CODI discovered late kills otherwise approved deals.*

Consent vs Clearance

Definition: Consent is agreement by a party to proceed; clearance is the legal elimination of that party's ability to block closing.

Perspective Notes:

- **Lender**: Clearance is required before funding
- **Borrower**: Often misunderstands the distinction
- **Buyer**: Must secure clearance, not assume consent

Why It Matters: Approval without clearance is provisional. **Deals close only when all veto power above equity is legally removed.**

Credit Committee

Definition: The internal body responsible for approving loss decisions and resolutions.

Perspective Notes:

- **Lender**: Accountability forum
- **Borrower**: Invisible gatekeeper
- **Buyer**: Ultimate audience

Why It Matters: Everything submitted must survive this room.

Deed-in-Lieu (DIL)

Definition: Voluntary transfer of property title from borrower to lender.

Perspective Notes:

- **Lender**: REO risk
- **Borrower**: Guaranty relief path
- **Buyer**: Often excluded

Why It Matters: DILs eliminate buyer participation but increase REO exposure.

Defensible Value

Definition: A valuation conclusion that can withstand scrutiny from credit committee, auditors, regulators, or investors using conservative assumptions and third-party support.

Perspective Notes:

- **Lender:** Approval threshold
- **Borrower:** Frequently resisted
- **Buyer:** Packaging objective

Why It Matters: If value cannot be defended later, it will not be approved now—regardless of price or urgency.

Deficiency

Definition: The remaining loan balance after net sale proceeds are applied.

Perspective Notes:

- **Lender**: Potential recovery or release
- **Borrower**: Primary fear
- **Buyer**: Cooperation lever

Why It Matters: Unresolved deficiencies sabotage closings.

Discounted Payoff

Definition: A negotiated loan settlement below the outstanding balance, not tied to a sale.

Perspective Notes:

- **Lender**: Loss recognition
- **Borrower**: Retention option
- **Buyer**: Competitive threat

Why It Matters: Discounted payoffs can preempt short sales.

Distress (Commercial Context)

Definition: A condition in which debt obligations cannot be met or refinanced under current market terms, regardless of asset operability.

Perspective Notes:

- **Lender**: Impairment question
- **Borrower**: Often denied
- **Buyer**: Entry condition

Why It Matters: Distress must be structural, not temporary.

Foreclosure

Definition: The legal process by which a lender enforces its security interest through seizure or sale.

Perspective Notes:

- **Lender**: Last resort
- **Borrower**: Public failure
- **Buyer**: Value destruction risk

Why It Matters: Foreclosure is process failure, not preference.

Forbearance

Definition: A temporary suspension or modification of enforcement rights.

Perspective Notes:

- **Lender**: Time management tool
- **Borrower**: Breathing room
- **Buyer**: Window creator

Why It Matters: Forbearance signals openness to resolution.

Guaranty Burn-Off

Definition: Provisions that eliminate guaranty exposure after certain conditions are met.

Perspective Notes:

- **Lender**: Incentive lever
- **Borrower**: Negotiation focus
- **Buyer**: Deal lubricant

Why It Matters: Burn-off paths preserve borrower cooperation.

Impairment

Definition: The recognition that a loan's expected recovery is less than its carrying value.

Perspective Notes:

- **Lender**: Accounting reality
- **Borrower**: Emotional turning point
- **Buyer**: Opportunity signal

Why It Matters: No impairment acknowledgment = no short sale.

Impairment Defensibility

Definition: The lender's ability to justify a loss to auditors, regulators, or investors.

Perspective Notes:

- **Lender**: Approval linchpin
- **Borrower**: Indirect impact
- **Buyer**: Packaging objective

Why It Matters: If the loss cannot be defended, it will not be approved.

Implied Foreclosure Bias

Definition: The point at which delay, escalation, or legal involvement causes foreclosure to become the default outcome absent affirmative resolution action.

Perspective Notes:

- **Lender**: Often unconscious
- **Borrower**: Usually invisible
- **Buyer**: Must be recognized early

Why It Matters: Once foreclosure bias sets in, optionality collapses and negotiated resolution becomes unlikely.

Intercreditor Agreement

Definition: A contract governing rights and priorities among multiple creditors.

Perspective Notes:

- **Lender**: Control document
- **Borrower**: Constraint
- **Buyer**: Clearance map

Why It Matters: Hidden consent rights kill deals late.

LOI (Letter of Intent)

Definition: A non-binding summary of proposed transaction terms.

Perspective Notes:

- **Lender**: Buyer credibility test
- **Borrower**: Directional clarity
- **Buyer**: First trust signal

Why It Matters: LOIs in distress must reduce fear, not excite.

Loss Defensibility Memo (or Executive Loss Narrative)

Definition: The internal narrative and documentation used to justify a negotiated loss over foreclosure.

Perspective Notes:

- **Lender**: Decision record
- **Borrower**: Indirectly affected
- **Buyer**: Primary submission objective

Why It Matters: Short sale packages exist to support this memo—not to market the deal.

Loss Mitigation

Definition: Any action taken to reduce lender loss severity short of foreclosure.

Perspective Notes:

- **Lender**: Mandate
- **Borrower**: Opportunity window
- **Buyer**: Entry condition

Why It Matters: Short sales are a form of loss mitigation.

Loss Severity

Definition: The total economic loss realized by the lender after resolution.

Perspective Notes:

- **Lender**: Primary metric
- **Borrower**: Abstract
- **Buyer**: Approval threshold

Why It Matters: Loss defensibility governs approval.

Non-Recourse

Definition: A loan structure limiting lender recovery to collateral, subject to carveouts.

Perspective Notes:

- **Lender**: Conditional protection
- **Borrower**: Often misunderstood
- **Buyer**: Cooperation determinant

Why It Matters: "Non-recourse" rarely means zero exposure.

PSA (Pooling & Servicing Agreement)

Definition: The governing contract dictating how CMBS loans are administered and resolved.

Perspective Notes:

- **Trust**: Rulebook
- **Borrower**: Invisible constraint
- **Buyer**: Non-negotiable framework

Why It Matters: PSAs limit discretion even when logic supports resolution.

Recourse vs Structural Non-Recourse

Definition: The distinction between contractual non-recourse and practical exposure.

Perspective Notes:

- **Lender**: Enforcement optionality
- **Borrower**: Often misunderstood
- **Buyer**: Cooperation variable

Why It Matters: "Non-recourse" does not mean "no leverage."

REO (Real Estate Owned)

Definition: Property owned by a lender following foreclosure.

Perspective Notes:

- **Lender**: Undesirable outcome
- **Borrower**: End state
- **Buyer**: Secondary opportunity

Why It Matters: Short sales exist to avoid REO.

Resolution

Definition: A negotiated outcome that settles debt, clears liens, and closes the transaction.

Perspective Notes:

- **Lender**: Risk elimination
- **Borrower**: Finality
- **Buyer**: Entry point

Why It Matters: Resolution—not acquisition—is the core problem.

Retrade (Commercial Context)

Definition: Any post-approval attempt to alter economics based on risks that were known, foreseeable, or priced at offer.

Perspective Notes:

- **Lender**: Trust violation
- **Borrower**: Deal destabilizer
- **Buyer**: Reputation killer

Why It Matters: Retrades reset approval, invite backups, and often terminate transactions outright.

Servicer / Special Servicer

Definition: An entity responsible for administering loans, particularly in distress.

Perspective Notes:

- **Lender**: Execution arm
- **Borrower**: Gatekeeper
- **Buyer**: Process authority

Why It Matters: Servicers control timing and access.

Short Sale (Commercial)

Definition: A lender-approved sale in which proceeds are insufficient to repay the loan in full.

Perspective Notes:

- **Lender**: Loss control tool
- **Borrower**: Exit mechanism
- **Buyer**: Basis creation

Why It Matters: Short sales are corrective, not opportunistic.

Special Servicer (CMBS Context)

Definition: The entity authorized to manage distressed CMBS loans on behalf of the trust.

Perspective Notes:

- **Trust**: Risk containment agent
- **Borrower**: Gatekeeper

- **Buyer**: True decision-maker

Why It Matters: Approval authority often shifts here without notice.

Standstill

Definition: An agreement suspending enforcement actions during negotiation.

Perspective Notes:

- **Lender**: Risk pause
- **Borrower**: Stability
- **Buyer**: Execution window

Why It Matters: Standstills prevent foreclosure momentum.

Standstill Agreement (Expanded)

Definition: A formal suspension of enforcement actions during resolution negotiations.

Perspective Notes:

- **Lender**: Risk control
- **Borrower**: Survival mechanism
- **Buyer**: Execution protection

Why It Matters: Without standstill, foreclosure momentum dominates.

Technical Default

Definition: A default triggered by covenant breach, maturity, documentation non-compliance, or economic infeasibility rather than missed payments.

Perspective Notes:

- Lender: Early distress signal
- Borrower: Often minimized
- Buyer: Primary entry condition

Why It Matters: Most commercial short sales originate in technical default long before payment default occurs.

Trustee (CMBS)

Definition: The legal representative of bondholders in a securitized loan.

Perspective Notes:

- **Trust**: Compliance role
- **Borrower**: Distant authority
- **Buyer**: Invisible veto

Why It Matters: Trustee consent may be required even after servicer approval.

UCC Foreclosure

Definition: A foreclosure on personal property or equity interests under the Uniform Commercial Code.

Perspective Notes:

- **Lender**: Speed tool
- **Borrower**: Control loss
- **Buyer**: Structure risk

Why It Matters: Equity foreclosures can bypass traditional real estate processes.

Workout

Definition: The process of managing and resolving a troubled loan.

Perspective Notes:

- **Lender**: Internal classification
- **Borrower**: Escalation signal
- **Buyer**: Entry stage

Why It Matters: Once a loan enters workout, resolution becomes possible.

Zombie Deal

Definition: A transaction that appears active but lacks impairment acknowledgment, stakeholder clearance, or timeline control.

Perspective Notes:

- **Lender**: Low priority
- **Borrower**: False hope
- **Buyer**: Capital and credibility drain

Why It Matters: Zombie deals consume time, stall momentum, and silently destroy reputation.

Closing Note on Usage

All terms in this book are used as defined here, regardless of industry colloquialism.

Where common usage differs by role, the resolution definition controls.

Appendix B: The Commercial Distress Resolution Lifecycle

(From First Signal to Permanent Clearance)

Purpose of This Appendix

This appendix exists to provide a **single, authoritative map** of how a commercial short sale actually moves from distress signal to permanent resolution.

The chapters explain *why* and *how*.
This appendix shows *where* and *when*.

If a deal fails, it fails at a specific stage in this lifecycle.
This map allows the reader to identify **where resolution is breaking—and why**.

The Resolution Lifecycle (High-Level)

A commercial short sale progresses through **twelve irreversible stages**.

Skipping a stage does not accelerate closing.
It causes failure later—at higher cost.

Stage 1: Structural Distress Emerges

Trigger:

- Maturity without refinance
- Covenant breach
- Capital exhaustion
- Rate cap failure

Key Reality: Distress exists before anyone admits it.
Primary Risk: Borrower denial; lender inertia.

Stage 2: Deal Selection & Early Kill Filters

Objective:
Determine whether resolution is structurally possible.

Key Question:
Is lender impairment plausible and defensible?

Failure Mode:

Confusing sponsor stress with lender impairment.

Stage 3: Pre-Foreclosure Access

Objective:

Gain visibility inside lender or servicer workflows before foreclosure bias sets in.

Key Reality:

Access is invitation-based, not sourced.

Failure Mode:

Outreach that increases perceived risk or workload.

Stage 4: Distress Confirmation & Narrative Control

Objective:

Move the loan from "uncomfortable" to "impaired."

Key Output:

Internal alignment that foreclosure is inferior to negotiated resolution.

Failure Mode:

Assuming price proves distress.

Stage 5: Short Sale Package & Committee Survivability

Objective:

Create a decision record that survives scrutiny.

Key Output:

A defensible loss narrative, not a buyer pitch.

Failure Mode:

Volume over clarity; upside over defensibility.

Stage 6: Buyer Strategy & Offer Control

Objective:

Be selected as the least risky counterparty.

Key Output:

Certainty of close that outweighs higher prices.

Failure Mode:

Aggression, retrades, or capital ambiguity.

Stage 7: Stakeholder Clearance

Objective:

Eliminate every veto holder above equity.

Key Reality:

Approval ≠ clearance.

Failure Mode:

Late discovery of junior liens, guaranty exposure, or consent rights.

Stage 8: Due Diligence Without Sabotage

Objective:

Confirm assumptions without resetting risk perception.

Key Rule:

If it doesn't change your close decision, it must not change the lender's view.

Failure Mode:

Escalating non-fatal issues.

Stage 9: Negotiation & Resistance Elimination

Objective:

Resolve all remaining friction before documents circulate.

Key Output:

Closing becomes the safest option for all parties.

Failure Mode:

Deferring "minor" issues to the end.

Stage 10: Legal & Tax Coordination

Objective:

Align economics with consequences.

Key Reality:

Borrower cooperation depends on legal and tax clarity.

Failure Mode:

Late CODI discovery; vague deficiency language.

Stage 11: Closing & Lien Release

Objective:

Convert approval into recorded finality.

Key Output:

Clean title, extinguished liens, enforceable releases.

Failure Mode:

Assuming closing is administrative.

Stage 12: Post-Close Value Creation

Objective:

Preserve basis, stabilize operations, and compound credibility.

Key Reality:

Lenders remember outcomes, not intentions.

Failure Mode:

Post-close chaos that erodes trust.

Lifecycle Truths (Non-Negotiable)

- Deals fail in order, not randomly
- Late-stage failures are caused by early-stage omissions
- Resolution is cumulative—each stage narrows optionality
- Speed without structure increases failure probability
- Clearance, not approval, determines certainty of closing

How to Use This Appendix

Use this lifecycle as:

- a diagnostic tool when deals stall
- a training reference for teams
- a checklist to identify missing work

- a reality check against optimism

If you cannot point to the current stage with evidence, the deal is not where you think it is.

Closing Note

This lifecycle applies:

- across asset classes
- across market cycles
- across lender types

Volume changes.

Process does not.

Appendix C: Kill Filters, Red Flags, and Early Exit Triggers

(How Professionals Avoid the Deals That Destroy Time, Credibility, and Access)

Purpose of This Appendix

This appendix exists to define **when not to proceed**.

Most damage in distressed commercial real estate is not caused by bad markets or bad pricing.
It is caused by **staying in deals that should have been exited early**.

Professionals are not defined by how many deals they close.
They are defined by the deals they refuse to chase.

This appendix establishes **non-negotiable exit criteria** that protect:

- reputation
- lender trust
- internal bandwidth
- future deal flow

The Core Principle

Short sales do not fail randomly.

They fail because:

- impairment is not defensible,
- stakeholders are misaligned,
- or execution risk is underestimated.

If these conditions exist, **exit early**.
Late exits are reputational events.

Category I: Structural Kill Filters

(Exit Immediately – Do Not Attempt to "Work Through")

These conditions indicate the deal is **structurally non-resolvable**.

1. No Defensible Impairment

Red Flags:

- lender insists value supports debt
- refinance still plausible
- maturity extension likely
- "market recovery" narrative dominates

Why This Kills Deals:

Without impairment acknowledgment, no loss can be approved.

Action: Exit immediately.

2. Borrower Can Cure but Won't

Red Flags:

- significant liquidity exists
- equity partners willing but slow
- capital call unresolved
- sponsor using buyer as leverage

Why This Kills Deals:

Lenders will not approve loss when cure is possible.

Action: Exit. You are a stalking horse.

3. CMBS With Unworkable PSA Constraints

Red Flags:

- no flexibility language
- servicer unwilling to escalate
- trustee veto risk
- rigid NPV test failure

Why This Kills Deals:

Logic does not override governing documents.

Action: Exit unless process certainty exists.

4. Environmental Uncertainty Discovered Late

Red Flags:

- Phase I ordered post-approval
- RECs surface after pricing
- Phase II implied without budget
- lender reacts defensively

Why This Kills Deals:

Environmental surprises reset approvals.

Action: Exit or restructure immediately.

Category II: Stakeholder Kill Filters

(Exit Unless Resolved Early)

5. Unknown or Hostile Junior Creditors

Red Flags:

- undisclosed liens surface late
- juniors refuse dialogue
- consent rights unclear
- borrower minimizes exposure

Why This Kills Deals:

A $50K lien can kill a $10MM transaction.

Action: Exit unless neutralization path is clear.

6. Unresolved Guaranty or Bad-Boy Exposure

Red Flags:

- borrower avoids discussion
- counsel delays language
- "we'll deal with it later"
- borrower cooperation degrades

Why This Kills Deals:

Fear creates sabotage.

Action: Exit unless addressed explicitly.

7. IRS or Tax Authority Timing Risk

Red Flags:

- liens identified late
- payoff timing underestimated
- releases assumed
- CPA raises late concerns

Why This Kills Deals:

Tax authorities do not move on deal timelines.

Action: Exit or reset expectations early.

Category III: Buyer-Side Kill Filters

(Self-Imposed Discipline)

8. Capital Ambiguity

Red Flags:

- conditional proof of funds
- committee approvals pending
- investor hesitation
- "we're confident" language

Why This Kills Deals:

Capital certainty is binary.

Action: Exit before credibility is damaged.

9. Retrade Temptation Exists

Red Flags:

- price feels "too tight"
- diligence likely to drive repricing
- underwriting relies on fixes not done
- emotional attachment forming

Why This Kills Deals:

Retrades erase trust permanently.

Action: Exit early or do not submit.

10. Timeline Control Is Lost

Red Flags:

- counsel drives pacing
- consultants delay
- milestones drift
- approvals approach expiration

Why This Kills Deals:

Delay increases foreclosure gravity.

Action: Exit before momentum collapses.

Category IV: Behavioral Kill Filters

(The Quiet Deal Killers)

11. Borrower Denial or Volatility

Red Flags:

- emotional swings
- blame narratives
- inconsistent cooperation
- threats or ultimatums

Why This Kills Deals:

Unstable sponsors create unstable closings.

Action: Exit unless borrower becomes irrelevant.

12. Lender Fatigue

Red Flags:

- repeated requests
- shifting contacts
- reduced responsiveness
- "we'll revisit later" language

Why This Kills Deals:

Fatigue equals soft rejection.

Action: Exit before credibility erodes.

The Reputation Rule

Every unresolved deal teaches lenders one thing about you.

Either:

• you protect process, or

• you create noise.

Noise gets remembered.

Professional Exit Discipline

When exiting:

• exit early

• exit cleanly

• exit without blame

• preserve relationships

Never:

• argue reality

• pressure decisions

• escalate emotionally

• threaten outcomes

Your future access depends on how you leave.

Final Test (Use This Before Advancing Any Deal)

Ask one question:

"If this deal fails six weeks from now, will my reputation be stronger or weaker for having stayed?"

If the answer is weaker, exit now.

Closing Note

Professionals close fewer deals than amateurs.

They also:

• waste less time

• lose less credibility

• get called first

• and compound access

Resolution skill includes knowing when not to resolve.

Appendix D: Resolution Artifacts & Required Deliverables

(What Must Exist, By Stage, for a Short Sale to Remain Closable)

Purpose of This Appendix

This appendix exists to eliminate a common failure mode:

> "We understand the process, but the deal still stalled."

That sentence almost always means required artifacts were missing, late, or weak.

Short sales do not progress on intent.
They progress on documents that reduce risk.

This appendix defines:

- what must exist
- when it must exist
- why its absence kills momentum

Core Principle

Every phase of resolution has a **minimum documentation threshold**.

If the artifacts do not exist, the deal is not "early."
It is unqualified.

Stage 1: Market Screening & Entry

(Chapters 1–2)

Required Artifacts

1) **Initial Deal Summary** (Internal Only)
   Must include:
   - asset type and location
   - lender identity and loan type
   - maturity date and rate structure
   - borrower posture (cooperative / frozen / hostile)
   - preliminary impairment hypothesis
2) **Capital Stack Snapshot**
   - senior lender

- known juniors
- guarantors
- obvious tax exposure

3) **As-Is Value Hypothesis**
    - rough market range
    - obvious impairment gap
    - known CapEx burden

Why This Matters

If you cannot summarize impairment in one page, you cannot defend it later.

Stage 2: Distress Confirmation

(Chapters 3–4)

Required Artifacts

1) **Inability-to-Cure Evidence File**
    One or more of:
    - failed refinance term sheets
    - liquidity statements
    - capital call failure evidence
    - rate cap pricing
    - DSCR projections
2) **Preliminary Valuation Support**
    - distressed BOV
    - relevant comps
    - cost-to-cure schedule
3) **Borrower Cooperation Confirmation**
    - data access granted
    - financials released
    - guaranty discussion acknowledged

Why This Matters

Distress is not declared — it is documented.

Stage 3: Package Construction

(Chapter 5)

Required Artifacts

1) **Executive Summary Memo** (1–2 Pages)
    - impairment explanation
    - foreclosure comparison
    - loss defensibility narrative
    - buyer execution profile
2) **Clean Financial Package**
    - T-12 (minimum)
    - rent roll
    - delinquency report
    - CAM reconciliation
3) **As-Is Valuation File**
    - BOV
    - comps
    - CapEx and rollover risk
4) **Buyer Credibility File**
    - proof of funds
    - entity structure
    - operator background
    - advisors identified

Why This Matters

Credit committees approve **files**, not conversations.

Stage 4: Buyer Selection & Offer Control

(Chapter 6)

Required Artifacts

1) **Resolution-Grade LOI**

    Must clearly state:
    - clean price
    - no-retrade language
    - realistic timeline
    - capital source
    - as-is acceptance
2) **Proof of Funds** (Current)

- liquid
- sufficient for price + buffer

3) **Execution Plan Summary**
   - diligence scope
   - timeline control
   - risk acceptance posture

Why This Matters

The LOI is not a price proposal.

It is a **risk profile**.

Stage 5: Stakeholder Clearance

(Chapter 7)

Required Artifacts

1) **Creditor & Consent Matrix**
   - every lienholder
   - consent required (yes/no)
   - leverage assessment
2) **Settlement Architecture Outline**
   - who releases what
   - deficiency handling
   - junior resolution path
3) **Title Exception Tracker**
   - identified
   - resolved or neutralized

Why This Matters

Approval without clearance is provisional.

Clearance requires proof.

Stage 6: Due Diligence

(Chapter 8)

Required Artifacts

1) **Defined Diligence Scope**
   - known risks only
   - no exploratory fishing

2) **Environmental Reports**
    - Phase I (mandatory)
    - Phase II only if pre-modeled
3) **Lease & NOI Reconciliation**
    - estoppels
    - SNDAs (if required)
4) **Insurance Confirmation**
    - bindable quotes
    - exclusions reviewed

Why This Matters

Diligence that creates uncertainty kills approvals.

Stage 7: Negotiation & Legal Coordination

(Chapters 9–10)

Required Artifacts

1) Deficiency Waiver Terms (Written)
    - explicit
    - conditional if necessary
2) CODI Exposure Analysis
    - CPA reviewed
    - exception path identified
3) Settlement Agreement Framework
    - releases
    - confidentiality
    - non-disparagement

Why This Matters

If consequences surface late, cooperation collapses.

Stage 8: Closing

(Chapter 11)

Required Artifacts

1) Final Settlement Agreement
2) Executed Lien Releases
3) Final HUD / Settlement Statement

4) Escrow Instructions
5) Recording Order Confirmation

Why This Matters

If it's not recorded, it's not resolved.

Stage 9: Post-Close

(Chapter 12)

Required Artifacts

1) Recorded Deed & Releases
2) Post-Close Verification Checklist
3) Operational Stabilization Plan
4) Lender / Servicer Close-Out Communication

Why This Matters

Post-close execution determines future access.

Final Rule

If the artifact does not exist, the **stage is not complete**.

Momentum without documentation is illusion.

Appendix E: Stakeholder & Consent Matrix

Purpose of This Appendix

Most distressed transactions do not fail on price.

They fail because **a required consent is discovered too late**.

This appendix exists to:

- identify every party with veto power,
- clarify what consent they control,
- determine when that consent must be secured,
- and define what happens if it is not.

Rule:

> If a party can delay, condition, or prevent closing, they are a stakeholder—regardless of whether they sit at the table.

E-1. Core Stakeholder Categories

1. Secured Creditors (Real Property)

Stakeholder	Control Type	Consent Required	Typical Risk	Resolution Tool
Senior Lender	1st mortgage	Yes	Deal veto	Sale approval
Junior Lender	2nd/3rd lien	Yes	Delay / leverage	Token payoff or release
Mezz Lender	Equity pledge	Yes	Control seizure	UCC termination
Tax Authority	Statutory lien	Yes	Super-priority	Payoff at closing

Key Insight:

> Priority does not equal cooperation. Every lienholder must be cleared affirmatively.

2. Secured Creditors (Personalty / UCC)

Stakeholder	Collateral	Consent Required	Typical Risk	Resolution Tool
UCC Lender	Equity interests	Yes	Post-close control	UCC-3 termination
Equipment Lender	FF&E	Sometimes	Removal / repossession	Release or payoff
A/R Lender	Rents / income	Yes	Cash-flow disruption	Assignment release

Key Insight:

If it's in UCC filings, assume veto power until proven otherwise.

3. Borrower & Sponsor Stakeholders

Stakeholder	Exposure	Consent Required	Typical Risk	Resolution Tool
Borrower Entity	Ownership	Yes	Authority failure	Resolutions
Guarantor	Personal liability	Indirect	Sabotage / delay	Deficiency waiver
Minority Partner	Operating rights	Sometimes	Litigation threat	Buyout or consent
GP / Manager	Control	Yes	Process obstruction	Removal / ratification

Key Insight:

Emotional stakeholders are still legal stakeholders.

4. Contractual & Operational Stakeholders

Stakeholder	Control Area	Consent Required	Typical Risk	Resolution Tool
Tenants	Possession / rent	No (usually)	Estoppel delay	Managed estoppels
Property Manager	Operations	No	Transition chaos	Termination notice
Key Vendors	Utilities / services	No	Disruption	Continuity agreements

Key Insight:

Lack of consent here won't stop closing—but it can destroy NOI immediately after.

5. Regulatory / Process Stakeholders

Stakeholder	Role	Consent Required	Typical Risk	Resolution Tool
CMBS Special Servicer	Approval	Yes	Process rigidity	Complete package
Trustee	Compliance	Sometimes	Silent veto	Early notice
Credit Committee	Internal	Yes	Rejection	Defensibility
Title Company	Recording	Yes	Closing delay	Pre-clearance
Escrow Agent	Funds flow	Yes	Mis-disbursement	Written instructions

Key Insight:

These parties don't negotiate. They comply or block.

E-2. Consent Timing Map

Stage	Consents That Must Be Secured
Pre-LOI	Borrower authority, sponsor alignment
LOI Submission	Senior lender receptivity
PSA Drafting	Junior liens, UCC lenders
Credit Approval	All secured creditors identified
Pre-Closing	All releases drafted
Closing	All releases executed and recordable

Rule:

A consent discovered after approval is a problem.

A consent discovered at closing is usually fatal.

E-3. Failure Signals

You are already in danger if:

- someone says "we didn't think they mattered,"
- a UCC search hasn't been reviewed personally,
- guarantors haven't discussed deficiency explicitly,
- borrower counsel "needs to review implications,"
- title says "we're still waiting on releases."

These are not delays.

They are unresolved vetoes.

Closing Note on Appendix E

Resolution is not negotiation.

It is **permission engineering**.

The Stakeholder & Consent Matrix exists to ensure that:

- no one is surprised,
- no one is cornered,
- and no one has leverage left to discover late.

Appendix F: Failure Patterns & Structural Causes

(Why Deals That "Should Close" Still Die)

Purpose of This Appendix

This appendix exists to strip away comforting myths.

Most failed short sales do **not** fail because:

- the buyer disappeared,
- the lender changed its mind,
- or the market moved.

They fail because **structural realities were misread, ignored, or addressed too late**.

This appendix documents the **repeatable failure patterns** that kill distressed transactions—and the **root causes beneath them**.

If you recognize a pattern early, you can still fix it.
If you recognize it late, the deal is already dead.

F-1. The "Approved But Not Closable" Failure

Pattern

- Credit committee approval issued
- Buyer proceeds confidently
- Closing never occurs

Root Causes

- Junior liens unresolved
- UCC filings ignored
- Guaranty exposure unclear
- IRS or tax authority not cleared
- Settlement language not finalized

Why This Happens

Approval is mistaken for clearance.

Approval is **conditional intent**.

Clearance is **structural completion**.

Prevention Rule

If a party can block recording, they must be neutralized **before** approval is treated as meaningful.

F-2. The Late Discovery Failure

Pattern

- Deal progresses smoothly
- One "small issue" surfaces late
- Timelines slip
- Confidence erodes
- Approval expires

Common Late Discoveries

- UCC lien on equity interests
- Partner consent rights
- Environmental history
- Title exception with legal impact
- CODI exposure

Why This Happens

Discovery is treated as linear instead of layered.

Prevention Rule

Anything that can surface late **will**, unless intentionally hunted early.

F-3. The Borrower Cooperation Collapse

Pattern

- Borrower initially cooperative
- Counsel enters late
- Resistance appears quietly
- Delays multiply
- Deal stalls

Root Causes

- Deficiency exposure unresolved
- CODI explained too late

- Bad-boy carveouts misunderstood
- Personal consequences minimized

Why This Happens

Borrowers agree to **economics** they don't yet understand.

They resist **outcomes** once explained.

Prevention Rule

Borrower cooperation survives only when personal exposure is resolved explicitly.

F-4. The Diligence Sabotage Failure

Pattern

- Buyer launches full diligence
- Consultants escalate minor issues
- Lender risk perception resets
- Approval weakens or is withdrawn

Root Causes

- Diligence scoped without intent
- Noise mistaken for prudence
- New third parties introduced post-approval
- Retrade signals sent unintentionally

Why This Happens

Traditional acquisition logic is misapplied to resolution deals.

Prevention Rule

If diligence doesn't change your close decision, it must not change the lender's.

F-5. The Advisor-Induced Stall

Pattern

- Economics agreed
- Documents circulate
- Advisors reopen settled issues
- "We need more time" emerges

- Momentum dies

Root Causes

- Advisors briefed too late
- No defined non-negotiables
- Risk elimination not framed as the goal
- Misalignment between legal precision and resolution finality

Why This Happens

Advisors are trained to **minimize liability**, not **close distressed resolutions**.

Prevention Rule

Advisors must be aligned to outcome **before** they review documents.

F-6. The CMBS Miscalculation

Pattern

- Buyer assumes flexibility
- Relationship logic applied
- Process rigidity ignored
- Minor deviation kills approval

Root Causes

- PSA constraints misunderstood
- Timing discipline underestimated
- Documentation not flawless
- Zero-tolerance environment misread

Why This Happens

CMBS operates on compliance physics, not negotiation physics.

Prevention Rule

In CMBS, certainty beats creativity. Every time.

F-7. The Closing Execution Failure

Pattern

- Deal reaches closing
- Administrative issues arise

- Recording stalls
- Approvals expire

Root Causes

- Payoff figures not locked
- Releases incomplete
- Funds flow unclear
- Post-close cleanup assumed acceptable

Why This Happens

Closing is treated as clerical instead of existential.

Prevention Rule

If it isn't recordable, it isn't resolved.

F-8. The Post-Close Reputation Burn

Pattern

- Deal closes
- Asset underperforms
- Chaos follows
- Lender access quietly disappears

Root Causes

- Basis squandered
- Stabilization delayed
- Aggressive leverage
- Over-promising post-close

Why This Happens

Resolution is mistaken for victory instead of responsibility.

Prevention Rule

The first 90 days determine whether this was a transaction—or a platform.

Structural Truth (Read This Twice)

Short sales do not fail randomly.

They fail because:

- veto power is misunderstood,
- incentives are misaligned,
- consequences surface too late,
- and execution discipline breaks under pressure.

Every failure mode in this appendix is **predictable**.

Every one is **preventable**.

Closing Note on Appendix F

If you experience:

- surprise,
- confusion,
- sudden resistance,
- or unexplained delay,
- you are not unlucky.

You are late.

Resolution rewards those who identify failure patterns **before** momentum builds—not those who try to rescue deals after it's gone.

Appendix G: Ethics, Boundaries & Professional Conduct

(What Separates Resolution Professionals from Predators, Tourists, and Burned Names)

Purpose of This Appendix

This appendix exists because **commercial short sales sit at the edge of ethical failure** if handled poorly.

Distress attracts:

- opportunists,
- pressure tactics,
- moral shortcuts,
- and reputational landmines.

Resolution professionals survive—and compound—because they understand one thing clearly:

> **Your reputation is always worth more than the deal in front of you.**

This appendix defines the **ethical boundaries, professional standards, and conduct rules** that protect long-term access, credibility, and deal flow.

G-1. The Core Ethical Framework

Distressed resolution is not adversarial by default.

It involves:

- impaired borrowers,
- regulated lenders,
- fiduciary obligations,
- public recording,
- and future scrutiny.

The ethical test is simple:

> *Would you defend this decision, process, and communication in front of a credit committee, regulator, or court—years later?*

If not, you are offside.

G-2. What Ethical Resolution Is

Ethical resolution means:

- **truthful representation of facts**
- **no manufactured distress**
- **no concealment of material issues**
- **no coercion through misinformation**
- **no retrade masquerading as diligence**

Resolution is not about exploiting weakness.

It is about **aligning reality with outcome**.

G-3. What Ethical Resolution Is Not

Unethical conduct includes:

- inducing default to create leverage
- misrepresenting buyer capital
- overstating foreclosure inevitability
- suppressing known environmental issues
- coaching borrowers to misstate hardship
- threatening exposure, publicity, or litigation
- using "buyer's remorse" as diligence

These behaviors do not just kill deals.

They **burn names permanently** inside lending institutions.

G-4. Borrower Conduct Boundaries

Never Do the Following

- advise a borrower to stop paying without lender counsel
- suggest bankruptcy as a tactic unless it is real
- promise guaranty relief you don't control
- minimize CODI or legal consequences
- "play both sides" without disclosure

Borrowers must understand:

- you are not their attorney,
- you do not control lender decisions,

- you do not eliminate consequences—only structure outcomes.

Clarity preserves cooperation.

False comfort destroys it.

G-5. Lender Interaction Ethics

Lenders operate under:

- regulatory oversight,
- internal documentation,
- career risk.

Professional Rules

- never misstate buyer capacity
- never imply approvals that don't exist
- never pressure individual decision-makers
- never bypass approval hierarchy
- never "shop" internal discussions externally

You are not selling a deal.

You are **supporting a defensible decision**.

G-6. Buyer Integrity (The Non-Retrade Line)

Nothing destroys reputation faster than retrading a short sale without cause.

Ethical Retrades (Rare but Real)

- undisclosed environmental contamination
- fraud or material misrepresentation
- incurable title defects

Unethical Retrades

- market softened
- leasing slower than hoped
- CapEx higher than modeled
- financing costs changed

If you retrade improperly:

- the lender remembers,
- the servicer flags you,

- access disappears quietly.

Certainty is ethical behavior.

G-7. Confidentiality & Information Control

Distressed information is sensitive.

Never

- forward lender materials casually
- share borrower details without consent
- use internal lender language externally
- leak deal status to brokers or competitors

Confidentiality breaches are **career-ending**, not deal-ending.

G-8. Advisor Conduct & Oversight

Advisors must be:

- competent,
- aligned,
- controlled.

Your Responsibility

- brief them early
- define resolution objectives
- prevent grandstanding
- stop late agenda insertion

If your attorney or CPA kills deals regularly, the problem is not the market.

G-9. Conflicts of Interest

Disclose conflicts early:

- dual agency
- equity participation
- referral compensation
- advisory roles

Hidden conflicts do not create leverage.

They create litigation.

G-10. The Long Game Test

Before proceeding with any action, ask:

- Will this reduce or increase scrutiny?
- Does this create certainty or fear?
- Would I want this documented internally?
- Would I want my name attached to this five years from now?

If the answer is no—**do not proceed.**

The Resolution Professional's Code (Summary)

You are ethical if you:

- reduce risk instead of shifting it deceptively
- prioritize closure over cleverness
- preserve dignity without creating illusion
- respect process instead of fighting it
- leave no unresolved harm behind you

Resolution is not about winning.

It is about **finishing cleanly—and being invited back**.

Closing Note on Appendix G

Distress will always exist.

Capital will always misalign.

Opportunities will always appear.

Only a small group of professionals will be trusted repeatedly to resolve them.

Ethics is not the soft part of this business.

It is the moat.

Appendix H: Illustrative Resolution Artifacts

(Annotated Structures That Survive Committees, Counsel, and Reality)

Purpose of This Appendix

This appendix provides **illustrative, redacted examples** of the core artifacts used in successful commercial short-sale resolutions.

These are **not templates**.
They are **structural demonstrations** of how disciplined resolution professionals communicate certainty, control risk, and preserve momentum.

> **Important Notice**
>
> These examples are provided for educational purposes only. They illustrate structure, sequencing, and intent—not legal advice, tax advice, or transaction-ready documents. All actual transactions require jurisdiction-specific legal and tax counsel.

H-1. Credit Committee Executive Summary (Annotated)

(The Most Important Document in the Entire Process)

Purpose

This memo exists to answer one question:

> *"Can this loss be defended?"*

Not to sell the deal.
Not to impress.
To make approval safer than delay.

Illustrative Structure

Transaction Overview

- Loan balance: $XX,XXX,XXX
- Proposed payoff: $XX,XXX,XXX
- Asset type / location: [brief, factual]
- Buyer: [entity + experience summary]

Annotation:

Opens with facts only. No narrative. Committees anchor on the first numbers they see.

Impairment Summary

- Loan maturity cannot be met under current market terms
- Refinance attempts unsuccessful (see Exhibits B–D)
- Sponsor unable or unwilling to inject additional equity
- As-is value below loan balance based on third-party support

Annotation:

Impairment is framed as **economic inevitability**, not sponsor failure.

Foreclosure vs Negotiated Sale Comparison

- Foreclosure timeline: XX–XX months
- Estimated foreclosure costs: $X–$X
- REO carrying risk and uncertainty
- Proposed sale provides faster resolution and lower loss severity

Annotation:

This is where approval is actually won. Foreclosure must feel worse—calmly, not emotionally.

Buyer Execution Certainty

- Funds verified and liquid
- No financing contingency
- No retrade posture
- Clean timeline and escrow discipline

Annotation:

The buyer is presented as risk reduction, not upside.

Recommendation

Approve negotiated sale subject to standard conditions.

Annotation:

No flourish. No persuasion. Just permission to say "yes."

H-2. Resolution-Grade LOI (Redacted & Annotated)

Purpose

This LOI exists to reduce fear, not to negotiate aggressively.

Illustrative Elements

Purchase Price

- $XX,XXX,XXX, as-is, where-is

Annotation:

Round numbers feel deliberate. Clever pricing invites scrutiny.

Earnest Money

- $XXX,XXX upon execution
- Hard after defined diligence milestone

Annotation:

Lenders watch when money goes hard—not how much you promise later.

Closing Timeline

- 90 days from PSA execution
- Extensions only for third-party delays (title, government)

Annotation:

Optimism kills credibility. Realistic timelines preserve it.

Contingencies

- Title and environmental only
- No market, leasing, or financing contingencies

Annotation:

Every contingency is a future argument. Eliminate most of them.

No-Retrade Statement

Buyer acknowledges pricing reflects known condition and risks and will not seek price reduction absent undisclosed environmental contamination or title defects.

Annotation:

This sentence does more work than a higher price.

H-3. Stakeholder Clearance Snapshot (Illustrative)

(The Veto Map)

Stakeholder	**Position**	**Consent Required**	**Risk Level**	**Resolution Tool**
Senior Lender	1st Lien	Yes	High	Sale approval
Mezz Lender	2nd Lien	Yes	High	Token payoff
Tax Authority	Senior	Yes	Medium	Payoff at close
Guarantor	Personal	Indirect	High	Deficiency waiver
UCC Lender	Personalty Lein	Yes	Medium	Termination filing

Annotation:

If this table doesn't exist by Chapter 4, the deal is guessing.

H-4. Settlement Agreement – Structural Outline (Annotated)

(No legal language — structure only)

1) Loan Payoff Mechanics
2) Release of Liens
3) Deficiency Waiver or Covenant-Not-to-Sue
4) Guaranty and Carveout Treatment
5) Mutual Releases
6) No Admission of Liability
7) Confidentiality / Non-Disparagement
8) Binding on Successors and Assigns
9) Survival Provisions

Annotation:

Vague settlement agreements don't fail at closing.

They fail six months later—in court.

H-5. Due Diligence Escalation Discipline (Illustrative Rule Set)

Escalate Only If:

- Issue changes willingness to close
- Issue creates uninsurable risk
- Issue creates incurable title defect

Do Not Escalate If:

- Issue was priced in
- Issue is operational
- Issue can be handled post-close

Annotation:

Diligence is not discovery. It is confirmation.

H-6. Post-Close Verification Checklist

Within 24–72 Hours

- Deed recorded
- All lien releases recorded
- UCC terminations filed
- Settlement statement archived
- Escrow holdbacks tracked

Annotation:

"We assumed it recorded" is how reputations die quietly.

Closing Note on Appendix H

These artifacts are not impressive because they are complex.

They are effective because they are **boring, predictable, and defensible**.

That is what closes distressed transactions.

Appendix I: Failure Modes & Postmortems

(Why Deals That "Should Have Closed" Didn't — and How to Prevent Repeat Mistakes)

Purpose of This Appendix

This appendix exists for one reason:

> **Most commercial short sales don't fail because of one big mistake.**
> **They fail because of a small mistake made too late.**

Appendix I documents recurring failure patterns observed across distressed commercial transactions — not hypotheticals, not folklore, but structural breakdowns that repeat across lenders, asset types, and market cycles.

This appendix is designed to:

- sharpen pattern recognition,
- inoculate against overconfidence,
- and prevent late-stage collapse after months of effort.

It is not accusatory.

It is diagnostic.

I-1. The "Approved But Didn't Close" Failure

What Happened

- Credit committee approval issued
- Buyer celebrated internally
- Closing scheduled optimistically
- Unresolved stakeholder surfaced late
- Approval expired quietly

Root Cause

Approval was mistaken for clearance.

Structural Miss

- Junior lien not fully neutralized
- Guaranty exposure unresolved

- IRS timing underestimated
- Consent assumed instead of documented

Prevention Rule

Approval is provisional. Clearance is final.

If every veto holder above equity is not addressed **before approval**, the deal is not real.

I-2. The Diligence-Induced Collapse

What Happened

- Buyer launched full-scope diligence post-approval
- Consultants escalated non-fatal issues
- New uncertainty introduced
- Lender re-reviewed risk
- Approval weakened and died

Root Cause

Diligence was used as exploration instead of confirmation.

Structural Miss

- No pre-defined escalation thresholds
- Consultants uncontrolled
- Buyer uncertainty telegraphed upward

Prevention Rule

If a diligence finding does not change your willingness to close, it must not change the lender's perception.

I-3. The Borrower Revolt

What Happened

- Economics agreed
- Legal documents circulated
- Borrower counsel surfaced CODI or guaranty exposure
- Borrower resistance hardened
- Closing stalled indefinitely

Root Cause

Consequences discovered too late.

Structural Miss

- CODI not analyzed early
- Deficiency language vague
- Advisors introduced after approvals

Prevention Rule

Legal and tax outcomes must be understood before approval — not discovered during documentation.

I-4. The Buyer Credibility Failure

What Happened

- Buyer offered strong price
- Proof of funds questioned
- Capital sources shifted mid-process
- Timeline slipped
- Lender quietly replaced buyer

Root Cause

Certainty was assumed, not demonstrated.

Structural Miss

- Conditional equity
- Committee-driven buyer decisions
- Soft earnest money posture

Prevention Rule

Buyers are approved as much as deals are.

Price attracts attention.

Certainty earns selection.

I-5. The Junior Lien Ambush

What Happened

- Senior lender approval issued
- Title review late-stage
- Junior lien surfaced

- Junior refused consent
- Timeline collapsed

Root Cause

Capital stack not fully mapped early.

Structural Miss

- Incomplete lien search
- Informal assurances relied upon
- No negotiated resolution path for juniors

Prevention Rule

A $25,000 lien can kill a $25MM transaction.

If a party can block closing, it must be neutralized early.

I-6. The CMBS Reality Check

What Happened

- Buyer treated CMBS like a balance-sheet lender
- Pushed for flexibility
- Missed PSA constraints
- Approval authority misidentified
- Deal stalled permanently

Root Cause

Wrong physics assumed.

Structural Miss

PSA not understood

Special servicer constraints ignored

Informal assurances over-weighted

Prevention Rule

CMBS deals are won before engagement — not through persuasion.

I-7. The "We'll Fix It After Closing" Myth

What Happened

- Issues deferred to post-close

- Releases incomplete
- Holdbacks undefined
- Title unresolved
- Lender refused to fund

Root Cause

Execution risk minimized too late.

Structural Miss

- Post-close cleanup assumed acceptable
- Releases not pre-cleared
- Escrow mechanics vague

Prevention Rule

If it matters, it must be resolved before funds move.

I-8. The Advisor Hijack

What Happened

- Advisors engaged late
- Attorneys reframed settled issues
- CPAs demanded restructuring
- Timelines reset
- Momentum lost

Root Cause

Advisors were not aligned to resolution objectives.

Structural Miss

- No early advisor briefing
- No defined non-negotiables
- Advisors incentivized to slow, not close

Prevention Rule

Advisors must be managed like stakeholders — or they become veto holders.

I-9. The Reputational Burn

What Happened

- Buyer retraded improperly

- Or overplayed leverage
- Or leaked information
- Or embarrassed decision-makers

Outcome

- Deal died
- Access disappeared
- No explanation given

Root Cause

Short-term thinking in a long-memory system.

Prevention Rule

Lenders do not forget. They simply stop calling.

I-10. The Final Diagnostic

If a deal fails, it almost always failed earlier.

Ask:

- Where was certainty assumed instead of proven?
- Which stakeholder was addressed too late?
- Which risk was known but deferred?
- Which conversation should have happened sooner?

Short sales do not collapse randomly.

They collapse **predictably**.

Closing Note on Appendix I

Appendix H shows **what works**.

Appendix I explains **why deals fail anyway**.

Together, they form the practitioner's edge:

- structure + judgment,
- process + restraint,
- certainty + humility.

If you internalize Appendix I, you will:

- kill bad deals earlier,
- close good deals more often,
- and protect the only asset that compounds faster than returns:

    ***Your name*!**

Notes

Notes

Notes

www.ingramcontent.com/pod-product-compliance
Lightning Source LLC
LaVergne TN
LVHW100315210926
848480LV00003B/1126

* 9 7 9 8 9 9 4 4 6 1 6 9 3 *